MIDLIFE CLARITY

USE THE LESSONS OF YOUR PAST
TO SPARKLE YOUR FUTURE.

ANDREA OLATUNJI

Charleston, SC
www.PalmettoPublishing.com

Midlife Clarity
Copyright © 2021 by Andrea Olatunji

First Edition

Harcover ISBN: 978-1-63837-089-5
Paperback ISBN: 978-1-63837-090-1
eBook ISBN: 978-1-63837-091-8

CONTENTS

WHAT IS THE STORY?

When people share their life stories in writing, gatherings, conferences, and podcasts, I have great admiration for their strength to overcome great traumatic events. I have seen incredible strength in people who overcame horrific abuse, ugly divorces, the deaths of children, being victims of violent crimes, and unimaginable natural disasters. The great strength people exhibit in the face of horrible experiences has often caused me to trivialize my own experiences. I have often compared my own daily life story to other people: "My life story and experiences are not as horrific" is one of the narratives I tell myself to express gratitude for having escaped childhood horrors. Soon, I started to diminish my own life experiences and the lessons I learned from them.

The stories that are shared among my group of suburban mom friends, when we really loosen up at dinners together, are breathtaking. One will casually share how she was abused physically, psychologically and sexually for a decade by a female relative, another will chime in with how she worked as a prostitute for money in college, another will remember the days she was strung out heavily on drugs both street and prescribed. One of my dear friends recalls the brutal murder of her sister by her boyfriend in their senior year of high school. One of my friends from college slept with our professor for three out of the four years of undergraduate studies, aborted a couple of pregnancies upon his request in her twenties, a couple of decades later, she suffers from infertility in her marriage, she is beyond consumed with guilt and grief about her past decisions. On and on I listen to intense stories of survival from women I know and read about, I have nothing overwhelming to share from my past. What about the present? One lady shared how she is cheating on her spouse with her college sweetheart and loving it, another will chime in about going through her day with wine in her coffee cup all day to cope with demanding life responsibilities, another one questions the paternity of one of her kids, and on and on in our nonjudgmental friendship. I often think I have to keep living to know what makes sense in my own life.

"I am no expert" is a narrative that limits me from sharing my wisdom; This narrative makes me minimize my perspective and the value I can bring to any situation. I take my own wisdom and experiences for granted.

It took me until my 45th year to embrace the wisdom in my own story as the gift in itself. My daughter, Oliva, was applying to a summer internship program in her junior year of high school when she came to the part asking her to write a short paragraph to describe how she overcame a hard situation. She was stuck and could not think of any time she had triumphed over obstacles. She literally said, "My life is not as horrible as other people's." I gasped because I recognized that narrative. Why compare your book of horror with that of others? Look at your own life and craft the lessons you learned while overcoming a hard situation. I reminded her of some of the events in her teenage years that had built her character. I reminded her of the hard things she had overcome. "Make a big deal of your own story," I told her. I painted her a picture of the past year. I reminded her in bullet points. I reminded her of when she was scared and pushed through, the times she felt sadness but showed up with a brave face, the times she was tired but finished strong, the times she shared her heart and risked being hurt, the times she slowed down to help others. "Your story is your story. Own it."

She wrote a truthful and powerful personal experience in her application. When she was comparing her story with her friend who had been abused and had suffered greatly, she was stuck in comparison. I saw the correlation in that moment. I, too, was trivializing my history.

History is full of nuggets of wisdom. Understanding and unlocking the lessons in the past experiences are what holds the key to unlocking the decisions and patterns of the future.

Your story is yours; it is a map to how your mind works and what needs to be tweaked. Observe your story. It does not always have to include doom and gloom to be a great story. Sit in your truth.

Reflect, meditate, and appreciate it. Your past deserves some of your time.

People often say, "Don't look back—you are not going back there." I say, look back at your story and the stories of people connected to you, learn from them, and apply your lessons to your future.

THE BIG QUESTIONING

According to the biblical writings of the book of Ecclesiastes, King Solomon, the wisest man who ever lived, repeatedly reminded us in his writings, "There is nothing new under the sun! Everything has been done before and it will be done again." The wisdom we seek in life experiences lies in studying our own story.

How do you tend to show up in conflict?
What are you afraid of?
What does your inner voice sound like?
What is your defense mechanism?
What is your coping mechanism?
Is fear a factor?
When do you know what you are doing is what you should be doing?
How do you know you are tapping into all of your God-given gifts.

Reflecting often is crucial at any and every age, but there is an even greater urge to reflect and sit in the questioning and full discovery of self. Meditating at what seems like the midpoint of life for me—45—is a good point to assess the journey. I want to share my lessons so that my daughters can learn some things early. If you can master some life dynamics early in your twenties, you can save yourself from some self-inflicted wounds. Heck, you can save yourself from unnecessary suffering! Life automatically has some built-in wounds. There is no getting around some traumas, but there are mindsets that are built to be powerful in spite of any level of trauma—a mindset that is truthful to self; a mindset that can honestly assess and ask the difficult questions.

What am I doing here? How did I contribute to this trauma? What is my contribution to my healing? What is my mind saying? What is my spirit saying? What is my body saying?

What thinking path and process needs emphasis, and which one needs to be extinguished for good?

For the past couple of years, I have been stuck on the same questions. I write them down in my journal, and share them with my spouse, my sister, and my best friend.

What got me here?

Is "here" a great place to be?

How do I know I am doing enough?

How do I honestly assess who and what I have become?

Should I always be becoming?

Should I sit here and simply enjoy my life?

Should I dabble into new adventures simply because it will satisfy a need in me to create something?

If I am doing a lot now, what makes me think doing more is the answer?

I have had these strong urges and questions of myself before. The last time I felt this was six years ago.

I have since trained for a marathon. I have created a women's/girls' empowering organization. I earned my yoga teacher training certificate. I turned all my energy to my family and tightened my circle of friends. Back then, my itch for change was to prove to others that I am more. This time, the craving is solely for me—a gauge in my soul, to check deep into my spirit. This one life! How is it going?

I have been training others physically, teaching yoga. I find that my words carry more weight than bulging biceps. I have been writing for years, but I have managed to tell myself the false narrative that "I am no writer" even as I penned it down on my vision board for close to a decade—I simply sat on it. I sat down to put pen to paper to define who I am now and what I want? NOTHING and EVERYTHING! I am content and hungry at the same time.

I know what I want from here, but not really. I want to create a black-owned fitness space, but do I? Maybe an aesthetic center, together with my husband? Nah. Maybe a tribal dance/yoga studio!

"How about finishing this book that I have been writing for a few years?" I recognize the gentleness of that voice. The strong nudge in my soul to go back to my original manuscript and get it out of my hands was undeniable. The universe kept showing up everywhere I went to tell me to get it done. The priest, the podcast, my fortune cookie, the random Instagram posts, and my yoga teacher all said it on the same day: "STOP PROCRASTINATING AND WRITE IT!" As if I needed clarity, on the same day, my daughter asked me what was taking so long in my writing.

"Focus on this one thing."

Keep it simple. What do I want, *now*? I have only imagined my future up until this point. I finished my education. I worked a few years in my field of study until I decided it's not what I want to spend the rest of my life doing. I have been working from home and the benefits of setting my own schedule have been priceless. I teach power yoga a few times a week at a local studio, I also enjoy teaching privately to some of my clients. This is more than ideal for me, but I know there is a nudge in me to stop long enough to finish this one thing. I continually pose the question to God, "What do you want me to do *now*?"

The still small voice in me says, "Just this one thing: Write."

The one thing that is hard for me to do is to BE STILL. Writing is not hard for me. I write casually every day. The first and only thing that I need to do is to be still and keep my promise to myself: Write.

Someone once said that procrastination is assuming God owes you the future— the future is now. Live in it-fully. I have felt this nudge before, and it created a different version.

If I die today, I would have lived a full, blessed life. But the purpose of living is to keep evolving by rearranging the thoughts and putting experiences into practice to serve the future of humanity—the humanity of even one person, because anything else can be crippling and overwhelming. I am tapping into a version of myself that I can look at in awe because that is the whole point.

Be still, and know.

ROOTS

"A tree's beauty lies in its branches,
but its strength lies in its roots"
—Unknown

The roots are where all the power of a tree lies; though invisible, it determines the strength, patterns and the possible future of the tree. In correlation to our human existence, the root represents the patterns of generations whose blood flows in our veins. Some of whom we have never met but the power of whose DNA is strong within us determine some of our uncontrollable variables. Looking back at our roots will help us to consciously lean on the traits we would like compounded and prune those we would wish to eliminate. There is immense amount of power in understanding our natural tendencies. Have you ever looked at the children in your family and see resemblances between them and the elders, past and living? The traits are not only physical, they can also be in the habits, disease patterns, intelligence, and drive.

DETERMINATION TRAINING

The older I get, the more I find value in studying my own behavior and those around me. I particularly enjoy getting to observe strangers, friends, and celebrities—not for negative comparison, but with deep inquiry. The universe is the biggest university if we stay in constant observation and study people, places, and things. School is always in session.

Why do I?

Why do they?

This is sometimes followed by "How" both in the positive and negative sense of the word.

Reflection is a sign of maturing: an awareness of what got you here and a great intention to navigate the future. I am not going back to the past, but forgetting all the lessons from the past is a waste of experiences. I say this often: A crisis, small or huge, is a terrible thing to waste. It's usually packed full of gold. Lessons, patterns, and habits can help navigate future tendencies.

I got all the way to my thirties before I took the time to start asking myself questions about myself.

Why am I optimistic?

Why do I have a heart for some things?

Why do I start some things and don't finish them?

When I was a newlywed in 2002, I would slice chunks of onions into my chicken when I cooked it. My husband, who hates onions, asked me why I have this onion habit. "Why not blend, grill, melt, and make the onion disappear and just enjoy the flavor?" he asked me. I looked at him like— I don't know why, I just do. My mom cooked like that. Her mom cooked like that. When he looked at me and asked me to change to better serve our new family's tastes and needs, my first reaction was to be defensive and feel slightly insulted that he did not like my style of wife-ing. It took some time to let the lesson sink in, but when it did, it took my mindset to a whole different level.

What else am I just doing without really thinking about why? How can I better serve myself and others today? If my cooking is influenced by two generations by default, what else am I doing like my grandma?

There is nothing wrong with tradition. I truly value tradition, but not at the expense of growth. Each meal I took time to cook was like punishment to my new husband because I could not consider cooking without sliced onions. It is not about onions, but what little things am I stuck on or, better yet, are stuck on me? I started to study my habits and search for the roots of them. Not just on big habits, but on small ones, too. Establishing what works to grow deeper into a version of me that shows up with vibrant branches. Asking "why do I?" has literally been a game changer in being a mindful human, not a mere zombie playing defense rather than offense in this game of life.

Asking "why" is the best way to grow deeper into self.

I was finding my roots, exposing them to life, sun, and fresh air.

I was the last child born into a loving family, preceded by a brother and a sister. My brother is nine years older than me and my sister is three years older. Each of us growing up in the same family with very different experiences makes me know without a doubt that your inborn personality matters to determine the lens you use to see the world. I have studied my own family of origin and that is helping me raise my own children. The contrast in how I saw my parents and how my brother described them is literally day and night. On the same dates, we saw opposites intentions and actions in the same people. As he grew older, he went even more extreme in his views. In recent years, his opinions are changing; he seems to be choosing to use a different lens to see things he had seen so differently in the past. Could it be that situations and how we remember them are based on how we were and not how it really happened? This has helped me to observe the narratives I tell myself and other people because it brings awareness to the state of my mind and soul. I find it fascinating also to observe it in people: the side and the tone of the story people tell tells me the state of mind they enjoy or suffer. But we are all a work in progress and we own the ability to change the lenses of our vision and the direction of our thought patterns.

The power to continue to transform is not in just accepting how things are, but our power, I observe, is in never stopping to inquire about the motives behind the thoughts.

I lived the first three decades of my life in what I call "Lala land." Thank goodness some things worked themselves out. I never questioned things. I just showed up and accepted what was. It's in my nature to be optimistic. It's my greatest strength and also my greatest weakness. I will look for the light in any and every situation like there is a reward for it. That's a darn good trait until you open yourself up to things that don't serve you and you cling to that one itty-bitty droplet of good in a sea of awfulness.

I developed a keen sense of questioning in my thirties, not to anyone else, but to myself. I find that questioning my motives gives me clarity to know that what I am doing is what I want to do. Initially, it was just an observation of myself. I was not trying to change "yet," I just wanted to get to know my own thoughts and motivations behind them. If I volunteer to lead a project, I get excited about it. I now sit with myself and inquire: Why do I want to lead or host? Why is this bringing me so much joy? Sometimes I found out that my reasons were simply superficially motivated by social acceptability or people pleasing, or being seen as smart and competent. Duly noted. No need to be defensive. Like rolling clouds, just observe the patterns and then with time and maturity, set the intention to correct if necessary—observation before correction.

As a parent to very diverse and unique personalities, I am more aware than ever of the need to appreciate every unique strength and weakness. They are the unique nature that often leads to life purpose. One is not more superior than the other. The task is to mold each child into their own maximum potential. Children who share the same experiences, parents, and relatives are so differently driven. What motivates one person is a stressor for another. Observing what makes each kid light up or what dims their light is an interesting appreciation for the uniqueness of each of the seven billion humans planet Earth must possess. Three of my four children are naturally mindful of their language and manners. I started to credit my parenting style to having such well-mannered children and might have even passed judgment on the parents with wild kids. But my fourth kid came for my self-righteousness. We have had more parent–teacher behavioral meetings and conferences for this one child than my husband

and I ever had in parenting the other three combined. Imagine the conversations with the principal about my kid's first-grade rap sheet, including multiple F-bombs and fighting bullies (and, yes, she is sometimes the bully). I observe her tenacity and resilience in getting her point across. That is her uniqueness—a world changer. Boldness is her unique thumbprint; she will need guidance and great investment of time, but all good things do.

As a yoga teacher, I enjoy the athletic, fast, intense kinds of vinyasa. I teach the same style I enjoy. Yet I am aware that the style of yoga I love so intensely is literally dreaded by others, while a slow, quiet class is like torture to me, but it's heaven to others. There might come a season that I transform in my preferences, but staying true is paying attention and not attaching inferiority or superiority to what I don't prefer. Others can have different preferences with no judgment from me. Observe the patterns in your thoughts, marriage, work life, and friendships. Pay close attention to the space between your ears. Give yourself full permission to change often. Put into full action all the lessons learned along the way and evolve.

DEEP ROOTS

The 1828 Merriam-webster dictionary describes clarity as a noun.

/Clar.i.ty/ The quality or state of being clear. Synonymous with transparency.

Sometimes I have to go back to pictures to capture the essence of the moment or the season. In the last decade, I thoroughly enjoyed taking pictures, not necessarily to share, but to help me remember the details of the moment. Of course, my family complains of me taking too many pictures, knowing very well they will sit together for hours laughing and enjoying the pictures and the moments around them in the future.

Growing up, there were four pictures of me and no videos. None. There was a picture of me as a 10-pound newborn in St. Louis, Missouri. The next picture was of my third birthday in Akure, Nigeria. Fast-forward to my next picture as a 10-year-old on my birthday, and the last picture of me was of my confirmation into my Catholic faith, which I guesstimate at 12 years old.

It occurred to me in my 45th year that I had no one-on-one pictures with my parents as a child. I have plenty of pictures with them as an adult—because I made sure I took a gazillion pictures. Cameras and capturing moments were not a thing for our family growing up in the 1980s. I remember tons of beautiful memories and making a big deal out of every birthday and holiday, but no one found it necessary to capture every moment as we do nowadays.

My parents are first-generation naturalized Americans. Both born and bred in rural Ondo-land in Nigeria, West Africa, they were the first on both sides of the family to travel over the Atlantic Ocean for the purpose of advancing their education.

My dad traveled first to the United States based on a brochure that he received that inspired him and his friend in the early 1960s. He was fascinated with cars—there were only a dozen cars in his village growing up. And he made it his business to take the cars apart and put them back together a thousand times.

My dad was born to a father who already had a family. When his first wife died, my grandfather married my very pretty, dainty, and barely of age grandma as a new wife. Not too long after, my dad and his baby sister were born. But then during a strong attempt to become a king in his hometown of Ondo town, my grandfather died suddenly. So as per custom of the time—wait for it—my grandma had to marry the first son. Did you get that?? My grandma married her stepson and had children with him!!! And that was completely normal. My dad's half-brother was now his dad. His oldest brother, Stephen, was now his dad. Stephen had a bad temper and he made it his business to beat the snot out of his little brother (turned son) Joe daily. Nothing Joe did was good enough. He was disciplined for just being. Dad recalled one time he was beaten, he wasn't sure what he did, but he was beaten so badly that when he peed, it was all blood. We assume that is why Dad was always a hard worker. He was always moving, cleaning, and making sure everything around him was straight.

Few people who grew up in that time period were educated. No one thought to travel outside of the town. No one craved anything more than the life they had, content with just farming and trading. While farming with his family, Dad saw kids walking to school. He was instantly intrigued. He was far older than those kids marching to school every day while he was laboring under the sun. He begged his mom to please let him go to school. She talked her husband into letting Little Joe go to school. He obliged and my dad recalls him saying, "At least I won't have to look at him all day, and he will still return home and do his share of the farming and cleaning."

Dad started school right away and that was the beginning of his life. He had never been so thrilled about anything as he was with school. He was older than all the kids in the school, so he learned fast. Math made sense to him. All the elementary work was easy and made sense. He had been doing them forever on the farms and trading cocoa, adding bags, taking away ounces of his harvest to make it affordable for buyers, dividing amongst farmers, and summoning all the courage to present his products for the day to his lunatic half-brother-turned-dad as his training ground for school.

He sped through elementary school, on to standard school, teaching his fellow students all along the way.

His half-brother/dad died young; the cause of death was not known. His mom later remarried and had more kids. But Little Joe was on an unstoppable journey of exploring life beyond what was presented to him. After he graduated teacher's training college, he was curious at the possibility of what could be next. He started working as a teacher in the teacher training college, where he found love. He sought out my mom, Florence. They courted, and he visited her parents. He was well loved by them. The only requirement from her family was that he had to join their Catholic faith. My dad had never even paid attention to faith, so he dove right in. He completed all the necessary steps and before you knew it, they were married in July of 1966.

What would be next? To everyone else, they were good to settle around town. Both educated, the couple would do well for themselves. But Dad had his sights on more. He wanted to further his studies. He was the resident engineer—fixing old cars, watches, or whatever he could lay his hands on. He applied to several schools.

He applied to schools near and far. His friends told him about a visa program that could take him overseas. He applied to it. He moved on with life with his new bride. They were pregnant within the first year. It was an exciting time for them. The new couple was close to the bride's family because they were simply more interested in their lives. My parents attended church with them, and my Grandfather Francis was well educated. The two men had that in common. Shortly after the newlyweds were settling into marital bliss, my dad received a letter from Southern Illinois University that they had come across his application and they would love to have him start the school year with them. They offered a student visa and accommodations. All he needed to do was leave his pregnant wife and his home and travel about 9,000 miles across the Atlantic Ocean to study engineering. The opportunity was great, but the timing was not optimal. The newlyweds agreed that he must go. Just like that, he became the first in his lineage to explore the world outside of what his parents had known. He became the first person in his history to get any level of education. He became the first person to reach for the unknown. He literally set the past on fire and faced the future. He was scared but moving forward. He wanted to see the pregnancy through, though; he wanted to be there for the delivery of what would be his first and only son. He wanted all of that. But more than that, he wanted a better life for the both of them—a life he could brag about. He wanted to be able to say, "I have never seen that before," every single day. He wanted his mom to be proud. He wanted his father-in-law to be proud of him, his accomplishments, and his bravery. He later told me, "Sometimes when you don't have enough courage to do something you really need to do, you really must just look ahead at who can genuinely be bragging about you once you get it done!" And that was a self-motivation tool he used a lot in his life. In this case, his mom would genuinely dance in the market, telling everyone how her kid is off to the "oyinbo-land," a land that is simply up in the sky. Dad traveled overseas.

Did I mention he has a pair of major tribal marks planted deep in each cheek on his face? You can thank his older brother/dad for that. He was about five years old when his brother/dad called him to the backyard where some firewood was already burning from dinner. Right then and there with no warning or anesthesia, he was permanently trademarked as a member of that small community. So fast-forward a couple of decades later, in the middle of his college experiences in the United States and his tribal mark forever became his icebreaker. He was much beloved because of it. Naturally, Americans were empathetic to his story and, before he knew it, he had created a large family of friends at school and before long, St. Louis felt like home. I wish he had documented every detail of their existence as Africans living in America in the '60s.

He wrote letters mostly to stay in contact with his pregnant wife, who had since moved back in with her parents until the baby was born.

The baby was born in February 1967. (Come to think of it—was that even nine months? Ooooh, looks like there was sex before marriage! I want my money back! Kidding! Not really!! Really!)

The baby boy was healthy, but mom had a complicated delivery, needing blood and several days in the ICU. She always said she was lucky to survive that childbirth in a rural town setting. They named their beautiful son Anslem Adeshole. The bond between the young couple was stronger than ever. The only logical plan was to unite the family. Dad started the application process for both his wife and son to join him. And very quickly, he got a response. His wife could come and join him immediately—she was even granted a student visa. But the baby would have to wait until later. This was bittersweet indeed. Of course, the adventure of life continues. Mom soon traveled over and Baby Anslem was left in the care of his maternal grandparents.

He ended up staying there for the first four years of his life. "Will that separation affect him at all?" was a major concern of Mom as she left for Missouri. She too adjusted well and studied hard. And they made great friends. The couple made a commitment to each other not to have another child until they were able to bring their son home to them.

There is a gray area where Mom does not like to talk about the time and emotional space between my brother reuniting with them in the United States as a preschooler and when my sister, Audrey, was born in 1972. Mom just greets the space with a sign of the cross: in the name of the Father, the Son, and the Holy Spirit. I never pushed her reservations until one day as Mom and I were casually discussing life in general while I was breastfeeding my third child. Mom stopped me in mid-sentence and whispered her truth to me: "I had an abortion before your sister was born; we did not want your brother to join the family with a baby added. We did not want him to feel like an outsider when his visa was granted to the States." My jaw was literally on the ground. No one was more Catholic than us. Growing up, we went to mass daily and I knew better than to not have a Catholic wedding. Mom's confession seemed like a load off her back. We both welled up in tears at what they had thought was sacrificial love for my brother. We continued our conversation in tears. She poured out her heart for the greatest act of her lifetime. I assured her of God's love and grace. I made her some ginger tea and we bonded over this deep-hearted conversation. I now never question Mom on why she wakes up like clockwork to pray the rosary on her knees at 3:00 a.m. daily or her daily 2:00 p.m. divine mercy prayers. She had not spoken of it to anyone before or since. She spoke it out of her mouth and the burden was lifted, though her prayer habits are stronger than ever.

As soon as it was possible, Dad went back to Nigeria to meet his son and return to the United States with the family together. There were so many struggles and wins along the way.

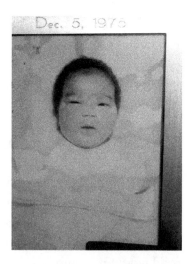

HELLO SELF.

Back in the '60s and '70s, when Africans came to the United States on a student visa, they studied, earned their degree or certificate, and got the hell out back to the motherland. In the spring of 1975, my mom was scheduled to graduate. My parents were ready to take their cute little family back to Nigeria to begin their professional careers. They were excited and hopeful about their future, which was full of possibilities. Imagine the shock of finding out that they were pregnant with me. I was due in December of 1975. It was the worst possible timing as they had already bought their flight tickets and were excited to return to see their parents, siblings, and extended family, and begin their brand-new careers. Their future was so bright, but the unplanned pregnancy was labeled high risk, so total bed rest was required. They were forced to stay in the United States for a few more months, and voilà! I made my grand entrance in December of 1975 after a heavy meal of Chinese pork and rice weighing in at a whopping 10 pounds via C-section. My parents waited the obligatory eight weeks post-op, but as soon as the doctors gave the okay, the Adedusan party of five arrived in Lagos, Nigeria, in February 1976, right in the middle of a military coup political take-over. The young family could not be deterred. They were determined. The adventure was about to begin. I lived my next 17 years growing up in Nigeria.

LEGENDARY PATTERNS

My husband often teases me about my childhood and my recollection of it—how I only remember and recount the same few memories over and over, or the way I have no details of what I ate, drank, or normal activities of daily living. I remember going to daily mass. I remember loving my maternal grandpa and how he doted on me. I remember being annoyed by my sister and her being annoyed by me always. I remember my brother was always in trouble; he was always running away from home and mom was always crying about him. I remember being called fat by the Oyinsan brothers and my dad telling me I was gorgeous. I remember my mom raising her voice at a police officer who disrespected her. I remember a random prophet who came into my dad's office and her prophecies that I was a member of some witchcraft tribe; I remember my dad kicked her out and reminded me that I was solid gold. I remember being so sad and scared when my grandpa died when I was eight. I remember we spent a lot of time with my maternal extended family. I remember my paternal grandma lived with us for a bit. I remember being so sick with malaria once that I passed out in the back of the car on the way to the clinic. I remember feeling excited about going to spend some time with an aunt for the weekend for the first time away and also my dad driving five hours to pick me up the same day because he could not let me go spend the night at other people's houses. I felt angered and flattered for the first time. I remember traveling to Canada with my mom in 1983 before my ninth birthday, my first and only vacation as a kid. Random things like that. But I know that I was loved, overly protected, and spoilt to a certain extent.

Growing up in Nigeria, it was typically considered a privilege for a 9- or 10-year-old to be accepted into a boarding school. I was looking forward to being admitted into some top federal schools where all the cool kids went, but my test scores were less than what was required for admission. I wished to travel far away, but as my fate would have it, I was admitted to one of the new schools only an hour away from home. (Major shout-out to my alma mater, St. Helens Unity Girls Ondo.)

I was one of the smart ones in school, but often felt rather dumb socially in current affairs, current dance moves, music, fashion, and so on. My friends often just ignored me in their "life" conversations, assuming that I would not add any value to most conversations. I had absolutely zero street smarts.

I started boarding school at age 10 and it was quite literally a shock to my system. I was hungry, scared, and felt inadequate, but within a month or so, I had found ways to cope by not worrying about the extras. I just did all I had to do to survive. I lost my bucket to fetch water, so I just bypassed the bathing process for about a month. When my parents came to visit on the allowed visiting days—the first Saturday of the month—they literally gagged at my appearance, thin and dirty. I clearly remember my dad scraping his nails in my neck and collecting old sweat that had gathered. What an experience! I realized I was not fooling anyone about my avoidance. My parents went to town and got me a new bucket and I committed to a mile trek to the reservoir to fetch water to bathe and wash my clothes. Things got easier because I adjusted to the new responsibility of taking care of myself. Resisting and avoidance of responsibilities only complicates simple tasks was the first major lesson the boarding school taught me.

I spent the lion's share of my most formative years from 10 to 17 in the all-girls boarding school—only returning home for a three-month vacation in the "summer" and two weeks' vacation each for Christmas and Easter. My dad visited more than he was supposed to legally; he formed a friendship with a couple of the House teachers. He brought groceries for them, and I found a bit of favor with the teachers in the sea of girls. Dad's eyes always welled up with tears every time he had to leave. I came to expect that look in his eyes, filled with love and admiration for me. That sure built some courage and reassurance in me. That look was gold all the way into my future; I lived to make his eyes proud. I said a lot of intentional "No" and "Yes" based on the memory of the trust in his eyes.

My mom was an authoritarian. She got stuff done and put me in check just with the look in her eyes. She was tough. We nicknamed her "Thatcher" for her no-nonsense approach to everything. She did not care about what we, (her kids, or anyone else thought; she was a true boss. She was deeply respected by our family and community for her strong mind. I didn't really get to start loving my mom until after I had my first child close to my 30th year. She did not leave any room or option for love—she was effective, but not necessarily loveable. She sent me to a boarding school with no lectures about menstrual periods or about the birds and the bees. Nothing. Just a clear, "Do not look at boys or you will find yourself pregnant." Which I took literally—I *literally* turned my eyes to the ground when any boys walked by anywhere. I really believed Mom. She was the best accountant, budgeting her way into a great retirement life. There was no tenderness in those early years from Mom. She was responsible and effective in "life." It all made sense as I got older. Mom is a reflection of her own mother.

My Grandma Emiola-Grace was born into poverty, orphaned early as a little girl. She had to prove her worth by being a helpful worker to extended family. She was not considered a beauty, but she was a fast learner in trading, farming, and selling. She was married off by a family elder to a rich older trader.

The rich trader happened to be impotent. Married for a few months, the marriage was never consummated. My teenage grandma kept her virginity and continued to be a diligent trader. Her husband kept trying to make love to his bride and continued to be unsuccessful. His frustration grew and he became violent toward his bride. One thing led to another, and her impotent husband went into an attempted suicidal-murderous rage. That prompted Grandma Emiola's family to return her dowry fees and release her from the marriage agreement.

She put all her energy in learning new petty trading. She was selling knickknacks and farm produce. She was not interested in being married off to anyone anymore. She was busy trading when she met my Grandpa Francis. Back in those days, in the Ondo culture, the girl had no say in the decision on who she married. The family decided who the suitor was and if he was suitable for the girl. Handsome Pa

Francis had been a player and was ready to settle down. He found my grandma attractive to marry but under the condition that she was a virgin.

He paid a heavy dowry for his bride, converting her to Catholicism. They got married and he had to confirm with the family on their wedding night that she was indeed a virgin.

She mastered petty trading, lived a full life, and died a millionaire at the age of 80. She was very effective, and never bothered to add loveliness to her repertoire; she got the work done. She left a legacy; she and my mom never hugged or said I love you, but then they had never seen it done in their lineage. They were successful and got the work done with no fluff added. Sharing the story of the women in my lineage is helpful to help me navigate the kind of woman I choose to be.

MY MATERNAL
GRANDPARENTS
PA FRANCIS AND
MAMA EMILYGRACE.

MY PARENTS JOSEPH
AND FLORENCE
ON THEIR FINAL
WEDDING ANNIVERSARY.

It gives me clarity. When you know better, you do better. The journey to betterness is never ending as long as there is life, there is room for better.

AWKWARD SPACES

I was 17 years old, freshly out of high school, when my parents made the decision for me to travel back to my country of birth to continue my higher education. They had made the same decision for my sister about nine months earlier. It was a decision they had made along with another family friend who had three teenage girls—we called ourselves cousins, because we were so fond of each other. The plan was to send us all as a tribe to a land none of us remembered but were privileged to have been born in. We can thank the 14th Amendment for that, I guess.

My sister and one of my cousin sisters traveled together a few months before the rest of us to live with someone's distant uncle for a few weeks, so they could get a small apartment of their own to get ready for my and my other two cousin sisters' arrival. What a unique life experience the upcoming season of life was!

I was so sheltered and incurious about life. I did not even bother to learn the currency, geography, or weather patterns of the United States. I just naively said "yes" to whatever idea was being thought up for me and went with the flow—no fear or worries whatsoever, just a sheepish "my parents know best" mindset. The rude awakening that I had in the months and years to come was a combination of a '90s comedy, drama, and some cringeworthy moments.

Our destination was Texas. Our parents had bought airplane tickets from Lagos to LaGuardia Airport in New York. They gave us $100 in 1993 for all three of us to find our way to Dallas, Texas.

Youth and ignorance are a beautiful combination. Ignorance is truly bliss. We were pumped up with excitement. We got to New York and were blinded by the beautiful lights. It felt magical. It was so far away from my boarding-school life. I pinched myself a million times to confirm my arrival into my future. I could do anything I chose! Wow! It was mind-blowing, indeed. I had no clear plan of what my future would look like, but I had wanted to be a doctor since I could remember—mostly because of the looks of approval on adult faces anytime I declared this. So my plan definitely included a white coat or bust! We rode a greyhound bus from New York to Dallas as joyfully as anybody could be, making friends with all who found our accents amusing. We arrived, spotted a pay phone, and waited another forever for my sister and cousin to pick us up because one of them was working and had to wait for the shift to end for the car to be available to pick us up. We were too excited to care about anything, but happy to have arrived. They had even arranged for us to begin working at the McDonald's where they worked as soon as the next day. Our Social Security numbers were pending but a job awaited. How bad could it be? I had seen Hakeem in the *Coming to America* movie. Is this my life? We woke up into working-class America early the next day. I knew I was in for a treat when the line was wrapped around the building with breakfast customers when we walked in. The young manager was excited to see us. He took a good look at us and split us fresh bloods accordingly. I got the unique privilege of being assigned to the drive-through lane as a cashier. He gave me a quick rundown of the "simple" menu. Yes, the menu was simple. But I got 99 problems and the menu is just one of them. What's a McSausage? Which is the dime? What is the nickel? It felt like an out of body experience in my 17-year-old mind. I was left for a moment to manage the drive-through cashier lane.

After counting up and down like a kindergartner, I was moved down to the "Can I take your order?" lane. I was only 24 hours on Texas soil, heck, in the USA; my accent was anything but drive-through ready. Try repeating Dr. Pepper back with the straight outta Ondo accent. It was awful. I was sweating trying to keep it together. The manager was annoyed at this point. He yanked me right out of that lane and within the hour, I found a non-speaking position, with a mop and mucky water. I relaxed a bit and decided to go back to the basics and study those—back to Sesame Street-level getting to know my new home from scratch, A to Z.

After that day, I never returned to that job. For one reason or another, the Social Security system delayed our cards for employment for about a month, which gave us plenty of time to soak up the culture and people. What does a 17-year-old girl do with all this freedom and no parental supervision in a whole new continent? It turns out my Catholic values had been cemented into my bones. I had zero appetite for the typical antics of a 17-year-old. I was homesick and filled my days with things I could brag to my folks about on our weekly calls. Dad would be waiting at the NITEL pay phone. It was 1993—the good old days with no social media or cell phones. I wrote letters—long ones to my parents to tell them the details of my moments. Once all my documents arrived, I worked two jobs. I thoroughly enjoyed being a wheelchair pusher at the DFW airport. My wage was $3.75 per hour, but there were heavy tips I earned for cuteness. I lived on those tips and I never even bothered to deposit my paychecks. We were late on our rent often because not all of us girls, who were roommates, would have rent ready. We rented furniture to own, but we did not pay on time and we watched as the furniture was returned. We sat with no furniture for close to a year. We learned that not all "no payments for a while" offers were worth it! What a gift my parents gave us: the school of hard knocks—five young teens thrown into a two-bedroom apartment to figure life out. An experiment in freedom and choices, but, luckily, it worked for us. We influenced each other, played, fought, and all came out on top. Learning the skill of diplomacy and human behavior as well as healthy and unhealthy competition was a life-long gift.

COMMUNITY

The key tool that molded us was community. Building a community from scratch. Meeting new people, getting to know them, and turning some into family. We were all so open to people of all races, gender, culture, and status. I remember clearly the first time we threw a house party in the good old 1990s. We were proud of ourselves, not for the food and drink that was provided, but for the fact that we invited all our new friends and they all shook their groove thang to our boom box. People are a resource—who would have thought it? We felt rich and loved by the joy and fun we got to share with people who sat around and shared the admiration for our accents from sunset till sunrise.

It was close to three months before we got all the necessary paper-work to be admitted into a junior college. It was enough time to start calling Arlington, Texas, home.

I learned that in life, the real you is who you are when no one is watching. My dad planted that seed in my head when I was little. I remember clearly, in primary school, when my classmates, a set of twin brothers called me fat and ugly, I was so saddened by the epi-sode—they even made up a jingle and sang it repeatedly to me. I cried so hard when my dad picked me up that afternoon from school. I was about seven years old. My dad looked me straight in my eyes as if I was being ridiculous and told me that I am brave, beautiful and smart. He reminded me to stand up for who I wish to be, even when I am alone. "Those boys were who they were when they were away from their parents, bullying a beautiful girl; they were sad and cowardly". I believed him. And that belief has shaped my entire lifelong self-es-teem. It made me very intentional about who I was at my boarding school when no one was watching. I would find myself talking myself out of a sad scenario and giving myself a pep talk. It made me want to be a strong, successful teenager in a western culture with no parental supervision. I simply wanted to develop a self I could be proud of.

I found myself graduating from a simple wheelchair attendant at the airport to foregoing my heavy tipping job for a more respected position as cashier at Host Marriott, a restaurant still at the Dallas/ Fort Worth International Airport. I worked the evening shift and sometimes a double shift because why not? I was saving to buy a car and I found a seller to buy a Mazda Protege from. I was excited to pay for it in nine installments. It was so exciting to negotiate my own price for the car. The seller was a young man who I realized later wanted to get under my skirt, but every time he made an advance at me, I negotiated a better deal. He was unsuccessful at his advances, and I got my first car for a steal. I was starting to recognize the power of me. Small amounts of progress led to an increase in courage to take on life a bit more boldly. I thoroughly enjoyed making my own plans and being successful in it.

I was registered for 18 hours of premed classes. I was focused, organized, and dedicated to my future.

At the end of my eight-hour shift, on a warm Texas night in September of 1993, on my way to go drop off the money bag and balance out of my register after a busy day at work, I spotted a velvety dark-skinned, lanky, lean body of gorgeous human in the airport train that took us to the manager's office at the end of the shift. He was wearing a green TCBY shirt. The time was sometime around 11:00 p.m. I stopped dead in my tracks when he smiled, and I felt the ground under my feet grow unstable. He was more beautiful than anyone I had ever met. His eyes were shy and kind. He waved. I looked away, embarrassed, when our eyes met. I snuck another look and he was still staring at me. We got off the train and went into the office. I pretended not to notice him in the office because I knew the managers would make silly fun of the situation and I did not want any of it. I was praying to God that he would not speak to me because I simply did not trust what my voice would do. As luck would have it, the manager was loud and carefree. "Have you two met?" he asked.

I looked away sheepishly.

The manager continued, "Michael, I think Andrea is from the same part of Africa you are from."

At this point, Michael jumped in and introduced himself and confirmed that he, too, was from Nigeria. We chatted about the specifics of his family origins. We even joked with the manager on the simple hellos and goodbyes of Yoruba language. I finished up my balance books first and said goodbye to Michael without exchanging contact information. Deep down, I really wanted to wait for him and talk some more. I wanted to ask when next he was working, what his schedule was, and when his days off were. I had a million questions, but my heart was fluttering. My face felt hot and sweaty. I said goodnight and nice to meet you and walked away. I ran to the train and ran to my car and screamed in excitement. I drove home in my Mazda Protege excited. I busted into my apartment and gathered my sister and cousins to tell them: "I have met my future husband!"

They shared in my excitement. My cousin Funmi was the most experienced and street smart of us five. She asked more questions, but I had no answers. But I was confident that Michael had love in his eyes. I went to the local Eckerd's drug store the next day after school to buy some makeup just in case I ran into Michael. I did not run into him for another six weeks. I started to think his good looks and my experience of love at first sight was all in my head. I was casually walking in the halls of DFW airport to deliver a key to a manager during my shift when I spotted Michael in his yogurt stand with a long line of people waiting to be served. He happened to look up at the same time, too. My breath left my body. He stopped everything and rushed to me. He said he had been trying to find me since that first night. He brought a napkin and pen and asked me to put my phone number on it. I gave him both my workstation and my home number. I felt like I was walking on clouds. He was real after all. By the time I got home, he had called and left his number. He called again and we have been talking since then. We were both premed students. So, naturally, we met up immediately at the local Country Kitchen to study for the upcoming tests. We studied till 4:00 a.m. He walked me home and we chatted till 6:00 a.m., knowing that we had classes at 8:00 a.m. We did that till the end of the semester. Michael got a transfer to my school and we became inseparable. He was a year and a half ahead of me. We transferred to a state college, UT-Arlington.

He got into Med school before he had a chance to get his undergraduate degree. I was obsessed with every aspect of him. He attended school in Galveston, some 300 miles away. I realized my dependency on Michael as soon as he left. I missed him terribly. But he was busy, extremely busy. This gave me time to find my feet emotionally. We talked every chance we got. Cell phones were not yet a thing in 1997–98. I, too, focused on getting my degree in Biology, spent a majority of my time studying for the MCAT. Standardized tests have always been my nemesis. I was so desperate to do well, but I fell short on my MCAT. After I got over the frustration and disappointments of the MCAT, I decided on other health field alternatives. It was easy at this point to accept—seeing how hard Michael was working—I was starting to doubt my own suitability for the field of medicine. I applied to the Respiratory Therapy program and I got in. I did not even know the roles of an RT. My need for change and "progress" was just too great to try the medical admissions again. It worked out. I enjoyed the field and called San Antonio home for those years. Michael and I commuted and grew into matured lovers. We would spend our weekends and holidays dreaming about our future, kids, and family dynamic. I loved him better with each passing moment and he in return simply adored me. We dated for eight years and promptly got married the weekend after his graduation from medical school. We started our married life together in Austin, Texas, in 2002. What a journey! That was four kids and a dog ago.

TRUNK

I visualize the human life as a tree. Giant or small, it consists of three parts. Roots, trunk and branches.

The roots are the early years and the influence of the generations before, the trunk is the middle where the individual gets to be formed into its own individuality based on environments, choices and life circumstances. The branches are the outward reflection of the health of the roots and the trunks and the possible legacy of what the future holds.

The trunk is the part of the tree that connects the leaf to the crown with its roots. The roots absorb water and nutrients from the soil, which are then transported up the tree trunk much like pipes.

The trunk section is where the experiences of life tends to hit us with no protection or coverage from parents or the support system the roots provided.

The trunk section is to equip you with the simple but powerful mindset to grow a healthy trunk and subsequently an attractive branch that you can be proud of.

Clearly we live in the information age. There is a wealth of information in your pocket, purse, or palm. Access to information is easier than ever. The access to great information is limitless, but also is access to distractions. There are a million ways to fill up your days with unplanned entertainment and cat videos. Be on guard on how you use all the information available to you. There is no order to the way life comes at you. There is an order your mind must be in to be able to sort out the difficult things when they come. I find that when any crisis arises, you must have a stored-up wealth of courage to face it. Gathering courage during a storm can be impossible. I noticed this about life. I observe other people's major crises and imagine the strength and mindset needed to weather the storm is not just roadside happenstance, but stored-up wealth in courage currency.

I read up on statistics, coping mechanisms, and human tendencies. Schedule your learning time into your day: 15 minutes a day to read up on a topic of interest can spark excitement into your mind. I use most of my driving time to listen to audio books. Add small doses of knowledge or wisdom into your bedtime, bath time, coffee time, and even quiet time. You never know when you will need to gather up courage from your everyday gathering of wisdom. There is hardly a Les Brown audio that I have not listened to or any of his quotes that have not helped shape my thinking in one way or the other. Not all voices or authors are appealing to my mind, but when I find one who is, I milk all the wisdom I can from their work. I read all their books and listen to their podcasts until I get an understanding of their great minds.

Keep seeking for wisdom and more wisdom. There are so many mentors to deepen the perspectives, knowledge, and expertise on various life topics. Keep studying people, living and even dead. There are so many lessons to be learned about various life situations that will arise. Learning is preparation of the mind for future situations. Build the muscle of the mind and keep it in tip-top shape because life gives no warning when it will drop a ton of weight on you to access your strength. The real flex is a strong mind. Stay ready.

TAKE NOTHING PERSONALLY

Not taking things personally is the most used characteristic I have had to develop as a grown woman, mother, wife, friend, and human. One of the agreements I have almost on a daily basis with myself is not to take anything personally. This one simple agreement has helped me to calm myself down in any situation. It works in any and all situations. It is not just a pie in the sky, but facts. The way people are to you is not really about you. The way they are to you is truly how they are to themselves. Lovely or hateful? It's not about me. What I must take personally is how and where I choose to insert myself in other people's stories.

My teen has an attitude! Not taking it personally helps me to see the situation without subconsciously making myself a victim of a disrespectful child. It really is not about me, but the struggle of the teen and probably wanting to be seen. Not taking it personally helps me consider the fact that teenage brains are not yet fully developed, so I can choose to step into the opportunity to help the thinking process—or not—without making it about me.

Seriously, make "Take Nothing Personally" the 11th Commandment.

Not taking things personally will let you come out of a conflict unbruised and possibly with more compassion without a need to give a piece of your mind. Not taking things personally allows the freedom to let whoever think whatever without the need to manipulate everyone's narrative.

All the times I have had regrettable actions were when I owned other people's insults and took them as my own.

A year or so after I finished my yoga teacher training, I was working so hard to develop a yoga program for athletes in a very meditative and restorative yoga studio. February rolled around and I was talking to a "friend" about how not many black people were attending my classes; I was looking for a way to promote yoga during Black History Month. She casually said because my products are "watered down." I literally felt a blow to my heart. Watered down? I wanted to cuss her and her whole lineage out. But then I breathed right through. That choice was not easy. What would have been easier was to give her a piece of my mind. But what good would that do? I moped around for a bit, took a long shower, called my sister, and enjoyed a cup of tea. I chose to not let her comments take any more space in my mental space. I chose to reevaluate my class and yoga practice to reflect who I am authentically. I adjusted my music to reflect my true self and brought all of myself to teaching anybody who chose me to teach them. There is a fine line between correction and criticism. I want to be able to identify my blind spot if I have one and correct it accordingly. Maturity requires me to sieve through correction and criticism without making an enemy out of the messenger.

I protect that real estate of my mind like my whole life depends on it. Because, frankly, it does.

There have been instances when I take things personally to the temporary detriment of my psyche. These are the moments that the mind and the spirit are conflicted. I know better, but I choose to engage anyway at the hope of a different outcome. These are times when my ego and my heart get in the way of being rational.

My family and I attended a church for close to two decades, literally the entire lifespan of my children's existence. My family, deeply rooted in faith, committed fully with our time, money, and relationships. While some people often get offended by messages from the pulpit, my family looks past the deliverer and claims that we have our eyes on God, not on the "man." Over the past few years, my teens started to bring my attention to contradictory words that were said and how the so-called "above all, Love" was not the message they were getting from church. I coached them to focus on God, not on the preacher, encouraging them not to take things personally. In 2020, after the death of George Floyd, a black man, by a police officer, Derek Chauvin, I was heartbroken and naturally expected the rest of God's people to feel the same. Black Lives Matter became an international debate. To my surprise, some church leaders went full throttle against Black Lives

32

Matter—how it was demonic and evil. I could not defend that based on the events of the summer of 2020. On the same day the videos of George Floyd's murder were released to the public, within the hour, some reputable faith leaders were already advocating on social media and on other publications the spotlight on good cops. Of course, Blue Lives Matter, but on the context of this day and moment in time, the focus of humanity, in my opinion was to weed out the bad apple that tends to spoil the bunch. Hatefulness and insensitivity had never been this glaring to me. I wanted to explain it away. My teenage daughter reminded me of the Maya Angelou quote: "When people show you who they are, believe them." My daughter added, "the first time."

I needed more time and evidence, I guess. I watched several Facebook live videos and it dawned on me that I loved the idea of a righteous church community so much that I stayed blinded much longer than I needed to. I tucked away every idea that did not fit into the narrative I chose to believe.

Black Lives Matter is not an organization to me, it's a phrase. It's powerful a phrase to encourage a fraction of us that felt overwhelmed with grief and fear. An assurance for the moment that we are all one. Kind of the same assurance all Americans needed to stay strong and encouraged after the 911 attack.

I had to protect my mind, protect my children's mind. The growth that needed to happen here is on me at this point.

I cleaned up my social media page and started the tough process of rearranging and cleaning up my belief system in real life. I needed to separate God and His church to keep my faith. I saw the business of the Church and I was disgusted. My kids! I felt like Sally Field in the movie *Mrs. Doubtfire* when she found out she had been fooled "all this time, all this time!!" I took it personally. I needed to be hit directly with a ton of bricks to get this right because I was so deeply rooted in religion. When the Insurrection of the Capitol happened on January 6, 2021, still in my feelings, I sent my former pastor a message to use this opportunity to address his past statements about Black Lives Matter. I wrote, "This is a godly opportunity for you to apologize." Why did

I need an apology to release myself from an organization? I took a business transaction personally. It really was on me to learn when and how I put blinders on.

When I see videos of any organization, faith based or not, expressing their views passionately, or with what I find insulting from the pulpit to describe some groups or ideas they disapprove of, I simply exhaled. I do not take any of it personally anymore nor the hundreds of supporters that cheer it on. The church has a business to run, and I now know better than to attach spirituality or eternity to business. The only choice I have is to remove myself where I no longer belong. Because the greatest betrayal to self is to see the truth and still choose to look away.

There will be so many opportunities daily to choose either to take any situation personally or see it for what it really was or a third option: None of my business.

NONE OF MY BUSINESS

A good "none of my business" approach will leave you liberated and detached from nonsense. Another 2020 moment: 2020 was really the year that came with free PhD training in human behavior and understanding.

I lost my father, I got stranded in Nigeria, Africa at the beginning of the global pandemic, and schools and businesses shut down. My husband was practicing medicine and I was worried sick about him bringing the invisible virus home. By the time George Floyd's death and the virus of racism was yet again exposed, it seemed like the emotional reservoir of all world citizen was low. There were worldwide protests to spread the simple message of "Black Lives Matter." I was shocked at the resistance against this simple message. I organized a prayer at the park to bring people of different races together to think up, because I frankly needed to think up. My children were looking for peace on Earth and I figured it might as well begin with us.

I noticed a tag from Instagram followed by a text from my friend in the ever-so-draining summer of 2020. It was one of the weeks when it seemed like white and black citizens of the world were having a reckoning. All the history of decades ago was coming back like a dam had broken. And it felt like a yelling race war. So the tag and text of my friend on a random Tuesday was more meaningful based on the climate and the tone of our world. I will call her, S.h.e, because the point of retelling is not necessarily to shame or blame, but to learn from the situation. S.h.e, a gorgeous white female, posted a beautiful message naming all the four black people she is in relationship with. My husband and I were two of them. The message warmed my heart. I remember stepping out of teaching a virtual yoga class to receive her message. It literally felt like a hug over the phone. We had dined together, run races together, and partied together. I truly love S.h.e. I expressed my heart for the beautiful message knowing that she will influence someone in her snow-white world. I was proud of her bold-ness to speak up at such a crucial moment in history. Within a couple of hours, just as I was beaming with pride at the love gesture, I busted out my phone to show my husband how amazing the message was. It had been deleted. My heart sank.

I took her positive gesture personally—it raised positive vibrations within me. All of me wanted to reach out and ask for the reasoning behind the deletion, but I held back. It was none of my business. I made it a point to make it none of my business. Whatever the issue is, she will have to bring it up to my attention. Hold your head high, shoulders back, and make some reasonings *none of your business*!!

And some situations are simply not deserving of any category. Just leave it alone.

I brought some food to a friend who was in mourning; and she proceeded to say, "Yes, thank you, I know you put a lot on Instagram, so thank you for the meal!" What? Is that a compliment? An insult? Should I punch her out? Should I hug her?

Nah! This called for a 'take nothing personally' and 'none of my business' combo.

The moment I go back to the foundational truth of not taking anything personally is when I can literally take myself out of other people's drama at least mentally, if not physically!

I had my first kid in 2004. One of my best friends traveled all the way from Dallas to Austin to see the new baby while we were still in the hospital. It was such an amazing gesture. She walked into the room and immediately expressed her surprise about the baby's skin color. "Why does she have to be so black?" It took me aback since she herself was a woman who was deeply rich in melanin skin tone, beautiful, and very successful. Even back then, I felt a sting in my heart and immediately decided to not take it personally. A friend who travels 200 miles one way for a day trip at the hospital definitely did not come all the way to throw insults around. Her experience is her experience. And my only job is to decide to care only for what's good for my child.

Not taking everything personally is the single best "trick" for in-law drama, political ignorance, racist nonsense, and on and on.

Letting things go is just a protective defense to keep the heart clear of hurts and hang-ups. If the other party chooses to amend, my heart is good and clear and if not, all is good. Life is too short for anything but fullness and joy.

Not taking offenses personally will require you to be able to school yourself into behaving up to your own standard instead of wishing everyone else does.

We called my mom "Thatcher" when we were growing up. She was tough and sometimes I wondered if she even liked us kids. She was a matter-of-fact kind of mom. That was the only way she knew to be a mom. Her mom was the same. My mom and I never had a one-on-one conversation until I was an adult. I was 18 and overseas before my mom expressed to me that she regretted not being more affectionate with us, her kids. She wished she told us she loved us and doted on us. She even apologized for it. I took that as a lesson in what to do with my future kids and to enjoy my mom as an adult not taking the past personally. My brother and mom have never seen eye to eye, and they both have the tendency to remember and recount offenses that are decades deep. My mom will tell you what happened on a Tuesday in 1910, down to the color of someone's blouse. My brother, too, tells stories of his childhood holding on to the offenses, personalizing them. Even now in his fifties, with his own family, he is sometimes held as a victim by the history that keeps repeating in his own mind, therefore holding him hostage from fully enjoying his life and sometimes hands down being destructive to himself and others. Good luck recommending therapy to an African family. For better or for worse, most likely the tools used for coping are religion or just a good ole "this is just me."

Maybe it was justified that certain actions done against you are awful. The business of healing thyself continually is what you take personally. I sometimes see some of my mom's tendencies in my parenting style. Sometimes, I find myself cold or too harsh when my kids are not living up to my expectations. I use those moments to remind myself of my lifelong work in progress. I do not take my moments of weaknesses personally, rather as a reminder to continually work on myself—slow to anger, slow to speak, and quick to listen. Some days are better than others.

It comes naturally to some to let things, good or bad, roll off their back. To others, they recount history like a textbook. Ego is a factor that I know must be released a thousand times a day to cope with some insults that people and life throw constantly and randomly. Let the ego go as often as possible. If someone gives you a side-eye, be oblivious to it. Do not take it personally. The more you love someone, the more the tendencies to want to take their stuff personally. It is not about you. The game of life is always going on in people's heads. From mere survival to trickery, learn this lesson: *never take anything personally,* good or bad. If you live by the praise, you die by the criticism.

RESILIENCE TRAINING

Merriam Webster dictionary describes resilience as a noun.

re·sil·ience
1: the capability of a strained body to recover its size and shape after deformation caused by compressive stress.
2: an ability to recover from or adjust easily to misfortune or change.

It goes without saying that 2020 is one of the most dramatic years of our era. Irrespective of location, economic status, race, age, or gender, 2020 came to whack all humans in the face and then proceeded to sucker punch some to a state of mercilessness. The degree of suffering caused by the global pandemic differs for all, but there is suffering nonetheless. I sit in reflection on my 2020 journey and I know the only way to take a giant or drastic step in any direction is to sit in this chaos. Chaos, like money, is an amplifier. It reveals the character of the person down to the root.

I must relish in the clarity of 2020. The perfect vision. The year that re-introduced me to myself. The year that I will always remember and possibly always be indebted to for giving me a new level of freedom to be authentically who I was created to be. The clarity I am sharing with you is personal and collective at the same time. There is no fluff. There is no time for fluff. I have lived half of my life if I am lucky. There will be no sugar coating on the lessons and clarity of 45 years and aha! moments because I have got to pinpoint some lessons learned, connect some dots quickly, and get to living the most authentic life, expressing the full range of who I am.

I have been a yogi since 2006 and I have been a yoga teacher since 2018; 2019/2020 is when I really got to practice yoga as a life-coping skill. Yoga off the mat is staying with chaos life throws out and choosing to be in the moment without judgment and discovering the good in the mess.

2019 was when both of my parents got ill. I, though the youngest in my family, got the opportunity to return the strength and love that both of my parents have poured into my spirit, mind, and body. Seeing the heroes in my life in an extreme state of weakness became a defining moment in humility and gratitude.

It was September 11, 2019, when I noticed that there was something odd with my mom as I was talking to her on the phone. She had been a caretaker for Dad. Dad had suffered from some mild dizziness for weeks. We had changed his meds and all physical examinations had proved nothing was wrong but old age. Just one more test, an echocardiogram to see the function of his heart, was left. I remember clearly; it was a Wednesday and just before lunchtime. I was picking up my kids from school when I made a typical phone call to my parents; they reside in Nigeria, West Africa, and I am in Texas, USA. Mom seemed overly chill and unbothered. That's when I knew something was wrong. I quizzed her: What day is it? What time is it? She was just too nonchalant. When I asked to tell me the birthday of her youngest grandchild, she just laughed out loud. I knew something was severely wrong. I called my brother, the lone sibling who lives in the same country as our parents, to call them as soon as possible and confirm or dismiss my fears. He called me back a few moments later to confirm that something was wrong. He was on his way to them, but that was a 4-hour trip. Thankfully, my aunt was there to assess in person and she too confirmed that things were bad. She said my mom did not care to keep the rent that her tenant just paid in a safe place. Oh shoot! This was bad. My mom doesn't ever play around with her money. She was later diagnosed with a massive stroke and spent a couple of weeks in the ICU. Dad was weak, but he was more worried about his bride of 53 years than himself or anything else. I booked the next available flight to see what I could do to help with the situation. It was not clear if either or both of them would make it through this health crisis. This is where the bulletproof yoga mindset came in to yoke my spirit, mind, and body. Whether life or death for either of them, I surrender. Nothing I can do more than what I can do; I did all I can do well. I advocated for mom in the ICU. I got her discharged and continued to dote on my dad, who was beyond worried about his bride. If anything happened to Mom, Dad for sure would not make it.

I took over nursing both of them. Mom had lost control of all her systems and was unaware of much. I initiated physical therapy with Mom, embolden by all the yoga training, my background in anatomy and physiology, along with respiratory therapy training. I incorporated some spinal, balance, and some band work. I sang songs and read books to both my parents. I cleaned up their spaces and organized their staff. I encouraged my family members to be brave. I called the priests to pray over them. I did all I could do. I did the best I could do. With no regrets and tears in my eyes, I returned back to the United States three weeks later to take care of my small children. And I continued telemedicine over the phone. If that was the last I saw of either of my darling parents, may God's will be done. I gave both of them a tight hug. That turned out to be the last time I hugged my dad.

SURRENDER.

Webster dictionary describes surrender as a verb.

/Sur.ren.der/
: to yield to the power, control, or possession of another upon compulsion or demands
: to give up completely or agree to forgo especially in favor of another

Surrendering is a mindset that can be implemented to opponents seen or seen.

A bulletproof surrender mindset is always there to tap into. Just breathe and be in this moment. After you have done all you can, simply stand.

With continued around-the-clock care, Mom recovered fully. She is still missing the memory of the stroke event and the fact that I came all the way to Nigeria, but she recovered fully. The doctors give credit to her otherwise active lifestyle of walking several miles a day and endless prayer and meditation.

We enjoyed another beautiful yet heart-wrenching few months, watching my strong, able dad slowly lose energy in his body. He had less and less appetite.

On February 6, 2020, my dad called me to chat and express his joy over me; I was impressed at his camera skills. I surrendered to that moment. He called me again before he went to bed; his voice was muffled, and I could not understand his words. But I encouraged him to get some rest and promised to chat again tomorrow. That was the last time I talked to my daddy. He died the morning of February 7, 2020; my brother called to announce that Dad died peacefully before his breakfast. I surrendered to that moment, too. I surrendered in tears and heartache, yet I surrendered. I reflected on his beautiful life. I read his autobiography that he had left for me out loud to myself, handwritten upon my request a few years back. I wept at the wonder of where his beautiful soul was currently. I wept at my own passing life. I wept at the meaning of life. I wept as I surrendered for what life would be without him. I surrendered to the unknown, believing that God was already there. I monitored my breathing and gave thanks to have been a beneficiary of such great love. I understand the benefits of yoga. I can hardly imagine coping without monitoring my breath. That the God of the universe knew about this very moment even before my dad was born. I reflected on his highs and his lows, his courage and his fears. I marveled like never before that the author of life, God almighty himself, took the time to make creation a mystery. I marveled that He breathed life into the intimacy of a man and a woman in a unique unspecific timing and at this moment marvel at the timing of death, how all his tasks on Earth were done. His task to me as my father is done. His task to his wife is done. His task on Earth is done. I wept as I congratulated him in my spirit and said out loud, "Well done, good and faithful servant. Enter into your rest."

HISTORY MATTERS

It was a Sunday night, March 29, 2020, when my friend D sent me a message from the United States. I was stranded in Nigeria where I had been visiting for three weeks. The visit was initially scheduled to be for 16 days. I traveled to Nigeria from Texas to bury my father, my dearest human. His passing even at an old age was deeply emotional for me. After all the burial plans and all the traditional festivities were wrapping up, there were rumors that the United States government was considering a self-quarantine for its U.S. citizens; it seemed unreal. A virus was spreading like wildfire all around the world: COVID-19 aka Coronavirus. Things started moving fast; the virus was spreading at an alarming rate! All schools were to be shut down. My kids, who were thousands of miles away in the United States, were to extend their spring break that is usually a weeklong even longer. And before we could even wrap our brains around all the new information, all international flights were canceled for a month—nothing in, nothing out.

When we (my sister and I) called the U.S. embassy on that previous Saturday morning to verify the rumors, they had nothing. Things were moving too fast. "Register on our website" was the only concrete information the U.S. State Department had for us. As soon as that phone call was over, I knew this was big. Whatever it was, was bigger than the giant of the free world can immediately comprehend.

I had traveled from Texas with my sister, leaving my husband and four kids at home. I had to play it cool to avoid spreading panic and anxiety. Surely that was not going to help anything.

What gave me constant reassurance was my brother who constantly reminded me that the U.S. government never abandons its citizens. He even reminded me of what happened some 20 years ago when as a young lady I traveled to the same Lagos Nigeria to visit family. I was bright-eyed and excited. But after the drive from the Murtala Muhammed airport to my brother's house, while I was off-loading my luggage, armed robbers busted into my brother's compound at gunpoint and robbed me and my family senseless—passport, money, and tickets were gone! He reminded me of how the U.S. government scooped me up and took great care of me!! That was 2000. This was 2020. Coronavirus was not a joke; the U.S. embassy shut down. China, Italy, and the United States were battling a rapid pandemic. And then several cases trickled into Nigeria. Within a week, there were close to a hundred cases in Nigeria and over 200,000 in the United States! And it was spreading, irrespective of class, age, and health status.

The U.S. State Department responded to taking us citizens back home. But they reminded us there would be a cost. And there was no set time for the flight, just get yourself and your travel documents to either of the two international airports cities in Lagos or Abuja and wait for further instructions. Electricity was not constant, Wi-Fi was impossible, so I turned on my roaming and bought data to use high gigabytes for hotspots so we wouldn't miss any emails or notices. We packed ourselves into my brother's house with his kids, my mom (because we can't leave the new widow alone in her home), and her assistant—so eight of us were living our lives in these uncertain times together. I had some cash with me in both currencies, but we had to live a very modest life not knowing when the flight back home was. Electricity was a luxury. I sweated like a fool and my bathroom uses were limited. My regular health nut routine of one bowel movement a day was nonexistence. The crazy thing was that my body adjusted to the stress.

I was in no mood for pleasantries when my friend in the first world texted me, "God is certainly trying to get your attention!" I went to bed that Sunday night with that on my mind! Why did he say that? I must get honest with myself. I was heavily bothered by his text. I think I am a great person. I think I am extremely consistent in being considerate of others. I think I am kind. Why did he say that? Am I being punished for something? Do I have a blind spot? I am really the kind of person who lives like it's my last day. I forgive, I apologize, I call myself out on my crap. So as far as I am concerned, I am living life well, but it's crazy how the mind takes off when you can't sleep, combined with the heat in a third world. What's next? Is this a test? Will my husband and kids be okay? And for the first time in my entire life, I panicked about trusting God. I did not panic for long, but the short time that night was intense and real. I was 44 years old and I had lived more life in the last 4 years than all the previous 40 years. But that's normal. Life really begins at 40. But then the more I dove in, the more I saw that there are no happenstances. Looking into the legacy of my heritage, so many choices got me here, so many sacrifices. I did not have the luxury of crumbling just because things were hard right then; I did not have control as to when I could get home, but I never really had control before. There is a God of the universe who is pushing things my way to make me believe I have control. I must know that when things are going against my desires, God of the universe is working even harder to make them so in order to protect my bigger interests. It was time to think, plant deeper roots connecting me to better things. No matter the process. I must trust that the Great Gardener cuts off every branch that does not produce fruit, and He prunes the branches that do not bear fruits so that they will produce even more. Those are scriptural red letters.

NATURAL PROGRESSION NATURALLY

I often tell my teenage son Noah, a Texan born and bred, an intellectual, and a very laid-back kid, when he is slacking off in his responsibilities, "Too many people have worked too hard for you to just show up to just be a regular average teen." I have a unique perspective of being a sandwich generation: looking at the sacrifices of parents and grandparents, evaluating my own life, and wishing the best for the next generation. It's a perspective that makes me want to rush the natural process of being a stupid, naïve teenager to tap into the meat of "what gifts are within him to move my generation and family forward?" But the natural progression of life must happen naturally.

YOUR PURPOSE; YOUR MEANING TO LIFE

I have been writing for many years but mostly for myself—mainly for therapeutic reasons, based on the season I am in. I typically have journals all around the house to pour out my heart. Oddly enough, I never fill one up before I start another. I don't keep them in chronological order. I keep a daily gratitude journal. In some tough seasons, I seek therapy by just breaking down walls within myself and being vulnerable to myself, not hiding the facts from myself. Faith and investing in the welfare of others helps me work through life situations fairly unscathed. When I experience life situations that I think are hard, God reveals a deeper version of myself and the more that is revealed, the more purpose is revealed to me. That season of 2020 helped me to build a stronger confidence in God as I witnessed all the systems crumble to an invisible virus.

There are always reasons to be grateful; things can always be better, but it can always be worse. Focus on the blessings in every situation to keep yourself grounded on what is important.

Just counting blessings will keep you on your feet in praise and your heart posture upright in genuine gratitude. Other people will look at you as naïve, but you are in a deep spiritual contact within yourself and your creator. If you never set foot in a church, mosque, or temple for the rest of this lifetime, do one thing: Count your blessings. Really slow your mind down to count all the things going right. Start with the very dependable sunrise and sunset. The sun hangs just right every moment as the Earth revolves around it. The precision of the creator is commendable. You don't even have to be any kind of spiritual guru to acknowledge this wonder. Slow down your mind enough to see the seed bloom to a beautiful flower, trees withering in the fall and like clockwork blooming in the spring. Wait just to pay attention to the next inhale, and then exhale deeply and intentionally.

When I was a college student in Texas, I traveled back to Nigeria to visit my parents. I cried so hard with despair at the state of humanity. I was helpless. I did the best I could with what I had, but I was discouraged knowing that it was a drop in the bucket. But I have grown up since then to not be discouraged but to joyfully do everything I can within my power. I cannot help everybody, but I can help somebody and that has to be okay with me.

Today, I just make it my business to bring what I bring. But first I must know what I bring. Taking the time to study myself to see, "what do I bring anywhere and everywhere I go?" has been a game changer for me. I don't want to just blend in and do what everyone else is doing. What unique qualities did God deposit in me? I have taken the time in several women's groups, my quiet time, Bible study, yoga training, family gatherings, endurance training, leadership roles, work environment, and even questioning trusted friends. The question is "What do I bring?" And then I go in and like a mandate from God himself, do that. I give allowance for transformation and change, but the core is always the same. My mindset is to take ownership for what I know is true. Acknowledged in any room or not, I am confident of the simple truths about me.

I know I am:

- Kind
- Generous
- Optimistic
- Faithful
- A leader
- Strong
- Forgiving
- Nonjudgmental (maybe a little bit)
- Open-minded
- Joyful

If you attack my character as mean, stingy, lazy, weak, unforgiving, judgmental, closed-minded, or grouchy, I am not even going to argue. I just go back to my intentions about the situation and make it right within myself. I have no need to justify my actions with everyone else, but I always need to check in with me. It really comes with age. I wish to speed up the process for my kids, but everyone has to find their way. It takes time for most of us to figure ourselves out—to not be concerned about being liked and approved of by everyone, but to seek to connect and be fully approved by the one and only compass placed by God himself within us. That is the work.

Self-reflection must be deeply honest. Light must be shed on the character flaw through self-observation and careful criticisms of a mentor or a deeply loved one. Personally I know I can honestly work on

- Being patient.
- Being organized.
- Being more detailed.

In some seasons, procrastination.

Being extremely honest with faults as well as strengths, I find it an effective way to catch myself when I am falling into undesirable patterns.

ESSENTIAL TRAINING

The essentials–

I attach God to people and people to God. When I wake up in the morning, I say my prayers, meditate on scripture, thoughts, and my breath. I pray to show up for someone as if God Himself did. I also pray to God to speak to me through people. I look for God in my everyday life. This relationship with the invisible God helps me to be in constant communion with Him but also to treat His creation with kindness. It's not as super-spiritual as you may think. It is very grounding. It's like a hug to my heart when it is so evident that God arranges people and events of everyday daily life to confirm whatever is going on in my heart. It's a never-ending communion. There is also immediate sadness or a quick nudge when I am unkind.

It felt like a God moment when I tuned in to Danielle's IG live while I was waiting for my daughter to finish up at soccer practice on a random Wednesday evening. Danielle mentioned a book she's reading. I did not catch the title; I texted her to get the title since I was looking for a good read. I chuckled as she sent, *The Essentialist*. I have been pondering on the word, *essential* for a few months.

2020 gave us essential workers. What is essential to me has been the center of my reflection moments. I am amazed at how random events, people, or places lead to complete inspiration and/or conviction. I met Danielle on Instagram and then we happened to be in the same yoga teacher training. What caught my attention about her is her badassery. I love her daily posts. The essentialist made me pose the question to myself, "Why are the most essential workers in our society paid the least?" It made me think that the societal norms are not necessarily in line with the important personal values.

It is essential to differentiate what is essential versus what the world rewards and then decide on who I am in reference to the standard—an intentional mindset set by observing myself and my tendencies rather than the cookie-cutter expectation for my demographic.

I was so delighted at the timing of the book. I immediately started applying the principles. I tossed all the items that were crowding my walls and closet. I painted my home to an agreeable gray and I noticed the energy shift even in my family at the minimalist approach. We started a toss or giveaway bag to avoid holding on to things that no longer serve us. I started to do the same thing mentally. What thought processes am I holding on to because it used to serve me, but much like the kids' clothes, I had outgrown. Equally important was to consider what thought patterns must be added to replace the old ones; better yet, enjoy the transition of an empty space for a while being intentional on if or what to replace old habits with. My entryway walls are still bare and I enjoy it like that for now. It had been crowded with beautiful family pictures for years. Once we took the pictures down to get the walls painted, the family agreed to enjoy bare space for a while. Even a minute change can be transformational.

It is vital to take constant inventory on what is essential in our own lives. What is worth spending time on? Who is worth investing in? Where do we get re-energized? But even more important is the re-evaluation of the things, people, and places we love every so often. Is this still serving us well? How can I make it better? How can I be better? Take experiences from the old joy and re-create a new joy formula as you evolve. I think this is what causes some of the biggest midlife unrest—feeling stuck with the old and the need to seek meaningful adventures. There will come a time when what is considered a blessing, if not nurtured, tweaked, or refurbished, will feel stale, unappreciated, and simply taken for granted.

I have been with my husband since 1994. It goes without saying that we are not the same people. The evolution of the spirit, mind, and body is certain. The adventure is to explore each other's new and evolving version, finding new, exciting ways for old lovers to be new is essential with each passing season.

I go in and out of seasons of wanting to drastically change and then stay in the new state for a bit and then repeat. From simple things like how I dress, to how I wear my hair, to how I cook, to how our home is decorated, to what fitness I dive into, to what books I read, to people I am with or choose not to be with. How I want to be made love to and how I want to give love. It's a whole evolution. I believe you can maintain curiosity just as day one of any relationship by actively studying the ways of you and exploring the ways of your lover. It is essential to me to keep exploring the minds of the people I want to spend time with but also not to hold them down to the old versions of themselves. Marriage is the real test of constantly checking in with yourself and your lover. A successful marriage to me is the study of the rhythm of the change, leaving room for growth, change, and finding ways to enjoy each other in the new version without suffocating the other with societal expectations. It would really suck to experience

49

love and life the way you did in 1994. That version of him and I have evolved two-hundred-fold.

UNIVERSITY OF "OTHERS"

No experience is ever wasted. None. The good people you meet and the not so good. The little hurt and the heartbreaking ones all serve a purpose to teach us something if we apply the lessons learned in the future. The universe of life has a way of teaching all the lessons if we are paying attention and studying consistently. Stay in the school of life, constantly asking yourself, "What can I learn from this?" Not only in the things that happen to you, but also in the things that happen to others. The strength they exhibit, the mistakes they make—"others" are the best school. I keep my eyes wide open even as I mind my own business. It has not always been so. As a young lady, I used to be fascinated in the juicy gossip of "who did what and to whom?" My motivation was for pure entertainment. Judging people for their unfortunate experiences or limited knowledge is a sport for the immature.

Maturity is when you hear other people's stories and you evaluate the possible characters in the story and observe their actions and make a mental or physical note of what you will do differently or what you will add to your "wise" box. Spending vast amounts of energy to judge others adds no value to your life. Extracting wisdom from others' stories is preparation for your future. When I read or hear other people's stories, I take serious notes because Life School is always open. Admission is open to all who will recognize its values.

My mom was sharing a story with me when I was a newlywed about my grandparents. Grandpa Francis was married to my Grandma Emiola-Grace. Grandpa was a sexy, tall, educated man, known in their small community for his good looks. Before they were married, he was the bachelor, sowing his wild oats. But being a "devout catholic," he settled into marriage and was committed to his wife (at least, that was what Grandma EG believed).

Grandma typically spends her sunrise to sunset at the market, trading, selling, and such. One day without reason, Grandma decided to go home for lunch and pick up an item she left to sell to a farmer later on in her day. When she got home, she noticed a pair of sandals she and her best friend had purchased together a few weeks ago at the flea market by the front entrance. Hers was still brand-new and unused in her closet. She got curious and entered the house with great caution. She approached the bedroom to hear the quiet moaning noises of her husband and best friend. This is where my ears were perked up to hear the rest of the scandalous story. Grandma calmly gathered what she needed for the market. She moved things around so that both her husband and her friend would know she had been home and for the win, she took the sandals at the front door with her to the market and proceeded with her day. I was eager to hear the rest of the story. Because my young self just knew, I would burn something all the way down. My mom told me the story so that I could see value in calculating my gains, losses, and future before I make decisions that will affect generations yet unborn.

Back to the story: a few hours later, as my grandma went on with the day, her friend took a walk of shame into Grandma's shop at the market and wept bitterly as she apologized for her betrayal with her husband. She confessed it was not ongoing but a spur of the moment error in judgment, yada yada yada. My grandma, so savage, simply threw her sandals at her and asked for an end in friendship and never to see her husband again.

My grandparents stayed married all the days of their lives. There is no documentation of how the husband and wife worked through the market sandal scandal knowing that it was probably the talk of the town. I wish my grandma wrote her state of mind down, that would be a great lesson in "how to."

The point my mom was making to me as a 26-year-old newlywed was to remind me that good people do dumb things. Sometimes you weigh the good and bad concerning your future before you make a decision that will forever change the trajectory. I tucked the story away in my mind as an unfortunate lack of power by my grandma. She had been born and raised in suffering was my excuse for her. But the more I live, the more I understand her reasoning. Her staying put in her marriage is not necessarily an easy way to address the issue. That was a great university for me to have attended tuition free. I tapped into that informal training more than a decade into my own marriage.

DETERMINATION TRAINING

There is an urgency in my soul to write. I have always been writing and shelving.

My closest friend Linda and I have been writers serving our community of women and teenage girls. We have written and shelved so many chapters. Every time we plan to publish so we can share what we know is worth sharing to help people, we get distracted by life and move on and hop on to the next thing. Our joint project is dope. It will be life changing.

There are simply some things that cannot be willed away. Writing this memoir is one of them; there are some things that cannot hide under the umbrella of partnership. You simply bite down the bullet and just do it.

Our unique mindset is our power. And the more I live and overcome life's hardship, the more I become even more confident that owning a strong mind is not automatic to all and I must share what I know. I want my own daughters to learn some things early and move on from milk to solid meat of life. Life is too short to be dealing with a childish mindset in the thick of adulthood. Wasting a couple of decades on lessons meant to have been grasped as a 10-year-old is like the biblical journey of the Israelites. Make the mistake, learn the lesson, and move to the next level of thinking. Repeat.

Gain access to the next higher order of thinking by constantly graduating to new levels of thinking. Rinse and repeat until Death.

Perspective and the posture of the mind matters in every situation.

Shortly after all the hype of New Year and a New Decade Resolutions of 2020, it must have been the 5th of January, after all the resolution buzz have settled a bit, Danielle presented a dare on her Instagram feed:

"What is one thing you want to accomplish that you want to cross off your list of accomplishments but also makes you sick to your stomach?"

That was a great question. I love reading people's responses to such questions. Most people want to lose weight, jump off a cliff, someone wants to adopt an international child, or someone wants to participate in a fitness competition.

The only thing that makes me sick to my stomach was writing and publishing this book. Not the writing part of course, but what if it is not valued as I think it should be? What if no one cares? I have had it on my vision board for years and I have had the same fear since then. What if it fails? What if I fail in it? After years of weighing and talking myself out of it, the only regret I will have if I die is not writing this book—and not getting a dog sooner than 2020 when Bleu, my miniature Aussiedoodle stole my heart.

A few years ago, I attended Catholic mass with my parents and the priest asked:

If you leave Earth right now, what is one thing you will look down or up from the afterlife and wish you had had the courage to do?

These questions are a great compass for how to spend our days. Let it determine what you think, say, or do. Let it determine your next move. Let it be an alarm clock to your soul. Let it be a great motivator to live life intentionally doing what you want to do rather than living in zombie mode.

Losing weight is not the reason to jump out of bed, but leaving a healthy legacy for your children's children will keep you truer to honoring your body, than popping some quick fixes.

Making more money is good, but a greater motive of building generational wealth will put a bit more purpose in your strategy of getting an education or a new certification or training. Your bigger motive will also make certain purchases unattractive. A $100,000 accessory might conflict with your long-term goal.

Attach long-term goals to your every day. How will you answer the underlined questions? Take time to be truthful. The answers will be your next mission. Adopt the swoosh logo of Nike. The swoosh is a simple design that is fluid and conveys motion and speed. The swoosh symbolizes the wing of the Greek goddess of victory. Just do it.

SHIP: SAFE AT THE SHORE: BUT NOT BUILT FOR THE SHORE.

I have learned from all the "ships" that life has put me in. And by ships, I mean:

- Relationships
- Friendships
- Leaderships
- Hardships

The ships of life, I notice, usually overlap. Hardships present themselves in relationships, friendships, and leadership. The skills required to navigate through life's ships is anchored in self-mastery.

"Who am I *now*?"

The "now" I find is the most liberating part of life. Freedom to acknowledge the past but not be stuck in it is a gift I find I get to give myself often.

Yoga teaches me this every day. I show up on my mat on a regular Sunday and my body beautifully goes into the complex "birds of paradise" strong and range of motion so unforced, but when I come back to the same pose on Tuesday, my body says, no way, not today. Move beautifully for the day, acknowledge and respect the "now." If I compare it with Sunday, it is a failure. The key word is *now*. If some of your thought processes from the past don't make you cringe, then you are not changing. Even the things you believe so strongly should evolve.

Naturally, I am a loyal person—loyal to a fault. I have had the same phone company and phone number for over two decades and the same bank account since I was a teenager. Loyal means consistency and stability to me.

It brings me a level of comfort to stay as is. As a child, we lived in the same house, went to the same Catholic Church. Subconsciously, I find stability in being loyal to people, places, and, sometimes, things. "If it is not broken, why fix it?" is my natural thought pattern. So I have had to coach myself to dig deep in my soul to ask, "Who am I now?" And dig deeper to, "Who do I want to become?"

In my stable upbringing, I remember vividly after my 10th birthday, my parents sitting me down and having a serious discussion that it was time for me to grow and develop a new way of thinking. I had just taken the common placement exams, a standardized test to get middle schoolers placed according to IQ. This is not an unusual process in West Africa.

My parents summoned me into a meeting; it was shortly after my 10th birthday. It was time to grow up.

I did okay on the placement exam. I did not get into my first choice of federal government girls' school, but once I got over the initial sadness of that news, I was excited to get into my second choice, St. Helen's Unity girls' secondary school. It was a boarding school. The meeting was to prepare me for what to expect in the near future. I would be living on the school campus for about three months at a time. My parents and immediate family could visit for a few hours the first Saturday of the month. This was all exciting to me, granted I had never spent a night away from my family. I just clearly remember my mom repeatedly reminding me that I needed to grow up, while my dad just kept looking at me like he was having second thoughts about the whole idea. I remember him comparing the experience to when he had to travel to the United States as a student and the pain his heart felt to leave his family behind—at least I was not going overseas was his consolation.

Well, it all made sense within the first week of school. The food was horrible, the schedule was strict, and the chores were unbelievable.

My heart ached from wanting to see my family; I was so homesick. I remember my first visit about three weeks later—my dad took a look at me and cried hard. "You are not eating well. Are you bathing at all?" I wish there were pictures of me in that season of my life.

After about a month of missing my family, I slowly surrendered to my new normal and started to adapt better. I started to look around and learn from other people. Even though the studying was rigorous and expectations were high, the most important thing I learned that first year was that I can adapt and learn so much from other people around me. My way of doing things or my family's way of doing things was not necessarily always the best choice. I can open my mind to different and enjoying differences were some of the vital lessons on that ship.

Shortly after graduation from high school, my parents and I had another life-changing meeting. "Listen, we can trust you and your sister to be able to handle yourselves with or without us parents hovering over you. We believe you should travel to the United States for your college education."

That sounds exciting, but we didn't have any close family anywhere in the States that I knew of. If my parents said it was safe for me, that was all the assurance my 17-year-old self needed. I believed in myself because they believed in me. Now that I have a 17-year-old daughter, what the heck? My parents were living on prayer. They were scared out of their minds to let us go. Mom was admitted to the hospital for two weeks after my departure to the States. Her diagnosis: high blood pressure.

Their decisions could have gone all kinds of bad and disastrous, but the power of the rosary, I guess. The two sets of parents prayed and trusted us five girls (now cousin-sisters) so much, we rose to the challenge. Ignorance is truly bliss.

I have a million stories of adventure from this season in my life. Even here, I ask myself, who am I *now*?

What got me here will not sustain me here. My boarding school experience got me here with coping mechanisms, but now I must build on it. I must read more. Assimilate into western culture while

I keep my sense of self. That took me a while to be okay with. I was conflicted for a bit because who I was, was not necessarily like anyone else. I was more quiet than normal because I spoke differently and the girls at work were mean. Girls in school were a bit more respectful and did not mock me like the girls at work. So I started to be freer at school. The more I expressed myself, the more I let loose and felt good in my own skin. I was able to distinguish between when I was forced to belong and when I was completely myself. And I simply studied myself intensely in this season.

I intentionally sought out situations and people who allowed me to express myself freely without pretense or being condescending to my personal values. I was experiencing real freedom—both physically and mentally. There was no parental or adult supervision, but the values instilled in my boarding school and perhaps my Catholic upbringing helped me to keep my head on straight and make decisions knowing the power of consequences and karma. Somehow, I knew the freedom I needed and desired was between my ears and there was no need to seek it in wild behaviors. I got a lot of satisfaction in those years by working long hours and taking 20 hours in college courses. I desired more than anything to make my parents proud. I stuck to my childhood dreams of pursuing medicine. Premed was my only focus. I studied day and night to keep my grades up. I only thought of extracurricular activities that would improve my résumé. It all went to a whole new level when I met the most handsome god at work, who happened to also be premed. It was a match made in nerd heaven. I told that story in the earlier chapter. I arranged to add a Respiratory Therapy degree to my Bachelor's of Science in Biology— all the while looking at my parents for signs of disappointment.

Not even a hint.

They were going to be proud of me no matter what path I chose. It was very important to me at the time to be able to pursue my life's adventures with no pressure. I liked the feeling of that freedom. I made a mental note of it. Michael and I got married eight years after we first started dating, and the weekend following his med school graduation—because you need a degree to be married as per an unwritten Nigerian parenting and life manual.

Michael was and still is the best decision I ever made. Being free in my spirit, mind, and body is important to me and also to him. So we get to enjoy being deeply committed to each other without a need to hover and choke out each other's need to breathe independently.

A win.

Random Light Bulb:
Complete Honesty Rarely Strengthens Friendships.

"END" IN FRIENDSHIP

Friendship is simply a gift that keeps giving because ideally you choose each other. The constant evolution of human minds is a factor that allows freedom in answering the simple question of "Who am I now?"

Too often, we start to demonize a friend simply because they are going into a season we are not ready for, or they are staying longer in a place that we have grown out of.

No one can force wisdom down your throat. And one person's lessons are not the other person's lessons.

Nonathletes and athletes alike can understand the analogy of a marathon, if only in theory.

In a race of 26.2 miles....

Everyone will have to develop a strategy to be able to endure the entirety of the race. Some will start fast and slow down later in their race, some will keep the same speed and tempo the entire course, some will do intervals, and some will walk the entire course. The important thing is to finish to get your medal.

Life is parallel to a marathon.

If you compare yourself with another athlete in the race, you are likely to lose focus on your strategy. Comparing could bring resentment, jealousy, or judgment of yourself or the other athlete.

Your personal best is not anyone else's personal best. Just run your own darn race with pride. Celebrate other people's wins without feeling horrible at your own attempts.

Comparison and unnecessary competition have been the demise of so many friendships and relationships—bringing an end to what otherwise could have been a beautiful fellowship. If a relationship does have to end at any point in time, it's important to end it in a civilized way. No need to burn bridges or set the whole experience on fire. We have no idea how the past and the future may connect.

The ultimate goal is to always be at peace with one's own soul.

I notice the things that tend to tie my soul down are bitterness, unforgiveness, disappointments, and regrets. You don't have to be a religious or person of faith to know this.

In *The Last Arrow*, Erwin Raphael McManus writes brilliantly, "If for no other reason, it's important to set your past on fire to set yourself free from all the things that you keep holding on to that keep holding on to you. And that doesn't go for just physical possessions. Set the bitterness on fire; light it up with forgiveness and watch it burn. Put the wounds behind you, put the betrayal behind you, put the failures behind you- or better yet, cut them into pieces, turn them into an altar, and let them burn. All that stuff is just baggage. It's too much weight to carry, and it will weigh you down and hold you back."

Amen to all of it.

A few years ago, we lost a family friend. Not to death. Not to any concrete reason that I can really tell you. We were closer than blood. We had been friends for well over a decade, since college. We did vacations, birthdays, holidays, dinners, dates, and pretty much everything. There seemed to be a natural shift. Naturally, we all evolve.

Just like that time when my parents said it was time to grow when I was 10, and again at 17, each time took me to a different level of awareness. The upcoming season demanded a transformation of me.

I had been busy with life—graduating college, getting married to my incredible human, moving to a new city, and having my beautiful children. Now it was time to summon my soul to wake up again.

What got me here, won't keep me here. There was a craving in my soul for something I could not identify yet.

In my 38th year, when my fourth child was still nursing, I picked up running. There was no spare time in my day and nobody I knew was doing crazy things like that. The right people were placed in my path to ignite this new passion. I met Shon on social media as she was forming a running group in the community. I did what I advised others not to do: I met a stranger at 5:00 a.m. to run. It turned out to be a divine moment. I could not get enough of the runner's high. We met three mornings a week, and then it was every day. I was getting fitter and faster. Soon I was leading others. I started to flirt with the idea of racing; I trained for a half-marathon. I was hooked. Talk about jumping out of bed kind of exciting. I came alive again. Most of my training was done before 6:00 a.m. I was walking on clouds. I was amazed by the power in my body and my mind. My spirit was elevated. The feeling was so good; it's safe to say, we were fanatics. Any typical morning, we would go for no less than five miles. We trained for speed, endurance, intervals, you name it—sometimes done with a dozen miles before sunrise. It was exactly the gassing up I needed. I understand why some people go through a midlife crisis. The kind of energy inside my body had to be expelled in a healthy way.

Running is a special type of therapy. A special time of devotion to your spirit, mind, and body. I legit write speeches to myself while I run, encourage myself, and reprimand myself—whatever I need to do to get the triad of spirit, mind, and body together.

December of 2015 was my 40th year. So to celebrate, I committed to training for a full marathon. It seemed like it was time to level up, to feel something I had never felt before, for my mind to grow deeper into its purpose, for my spirit to radiate all the goodness it can potentially accommodate at this stage of life.

Growing with purpose beats being forced by life to grow and change. Because either way, change is inevitable.

The training leading to the Dallas marathon was definitely life changing. I got bolder and stronger. The need to please others seemed to diminish. I checked in with myself often and I felt like I was floating on cloud nine. Race day was the mother of all teachers. I started steady, but slowed down a little at mile 10 to pace myself. I felt like quitting on mile 15. I found some of my cheerleaders on mile 16, and kept going, but the thought of 10 more miles to the finish line was like death to me. My friends showed up and were running beside me at this point. The pride of not letting them down kept me up and going for a bit. Then somewhere between mile 20 and 21, I dropped to my knee. I was done. "God, please let someone put me on a stretcher so I don't die on this asphalt."

I needed a miracle, and I promise you, that is exactly what I got. I looked up to decide what spot to hang my heavy head. And right there, with signs in their hands, were my kids and husband. I thought, "Darn it!! Why do they have to be here, the moment I have just the strength to want to die?" My friends helped me to the sidewalk; my husband offered me the protein drink I had prepared at home earlier that morning. I chugged it down. I allowed some fresh air into my lungs. I waited a moment, and assessed myself to see how I felt. I got up with extra electrolytes and protein in my body. Let's go! There were about five miles to the finish line. My oldest daughter, Olivia, who was about 11 at the time, offered to finish with me.

So, with friends and my daughter in place, we walked, jogged, prayed, sang, and even made jokes all the way to that finish line. And even though my body was weak, my heart was too full. Overflowing with too many emotions and lessons. That very day, I transformed to a deeper version of me. The person I could look up to. I found the power in beautiful friendships and community. I found the power within me that I can trust to finish strong, to see hard and believe I could—not in a poetic wishful way—really crush hard situations and still maintain myself. I found a woman within me who can weather the storm and not become "mean" or seek "pity." I found the woman I could admire. I can trust me—bold, strong, badass, and soft at heart. I found a hero within myself! My children were there to see it all. That was a moment! There were no words at the finish line. Just hugs, tears, and a look on my very introverted son's face that says it all. "She is mad crazy, and she is my mother!"

I went to see my doctor for my annual checkup a few days after the big race; I was still so spent. She called me back within the hour and urged me to have someone drive me in for a blood transfusion. My blood count was extremely low. My iron and hemoglobin was dangerously low. She wondered how I was walking around with those numbers. I was so excited when she said that, mostly because it explained the reason for my near-death experience! I refused the blood transfusions but was grateful for a prescription for a good iron supplement! I doubled up on my spinach and red meat intake and gave my body time to normalize.

Back to the "end" in our friendship. My new passion for running has dampened our season of friendship. I didn't really notice until hindsight. After my race, I joined the vitamin selling company; I was using it for overall health and wellness and I attempted to convince my friends to support my new venture. Nothing kills a friendship faster than multilevel marketing.

My excitement was received adversely. I was probably high on life or running and was no humble pie. I took their coldness personally. I was angry at them because my expectations of them were automatic, and I told them the way I want to be told "too much truth!"

This was the end of our beautiful friendSHIP. Within a day after our come to Jesus, truthful confrontation, I apologized, begged, cried, mourned, and begged again. I wrote apology texts. I invited myself and my kids over. I did too much to mend this "ship"! But it was beyond repair. It took me well over a year to get over this loss. And, finally, I just had to put it six feet under, mourn for as long as I needed, while I wished them well, releasing all bitterness, unforgiveness, and regrets. This loss taught me the most about human behavior to date. It also taught me the most about myself and offered so many lessons. I was sad for my kids who lost their friends, too. So when we see our old friends around town, I remind the kids of all the beautiful times we got to share together.

Leaving no room for bitterness is the gift you simply must give yourself in any life situation. Acknowledge your part in the breakdown, release the past, and look ahead "with great excitement" for what the future holds. Because life comes in seasons.

A Chinese proverb compares friends to the jaws and teeth of a dangerous animal—if you are not careful, you will find them chewing you up. Tell yourself the truth if you are the friend who chewed others up. When emotions overcome logic and reasoning, relationships are destroyed.

I am usually honey to situations, but with maturity, I started to own the part of any relationship in which I caused the breakdown because of my salty ways.

Are you always a hero in your life story? Find the scenario in your own life in which you behaved badly. Acknowledge your own faults.

Maturity.

WORST DAYS: BEST SCHOOL.

2015–2016 was a very dramatic season for our marriage. Michael had been practicing medicine for a decade. I became his practice manager, which afforded me the privilege of working from home. I had not practiced my trade of Respiratory Therapy since our son was born a decade ago. Our family, a party of six, was complete. It was a smooth season until we were rudely interrupted by a registered mail at our front door. Michael had been named in a lawsuit! To say he was devastated would be an understatement. Medicine was his passion, calling, identity, and his bread and butter. He read through the accusations and charts, and he was confident he had done nothing wrong. His medical malpractice attorney assured him it was just a money grab. He did not do anything wrong, "an easy case" for them. He was named with a bunch of other physicians and the hospital. He was advised not to settle out of court, plus that will put a speck on his squeaky clean medical practice record.

"Trial will be the easy way out!" was the advice.

Wrong!

Trial was horrible. People lie. People cheat. Experts lie. The case was lost after Michael spent more than eight hours a day at the court for more than eight weeks of testimony, while practicing medicine daily. The season was exhausting. We just stayed in it, heads down, butts up.

I supported my husband by maintaining a good pace at the home front. I took care of all the extracurricular activities, not stressing Michael about being at any sporting events. He was knee-deep with life, and I naturally wanted to protect his emotions. Thankfully, running was therapy. There was no idle time. My running group once met up at 2:00 a.m. for a training run. I think we ran 14 miles and got back home before 6:00 a.m., when kids would need to start getting ready for school. Laser focused, I had too much energy pinned inside because of the daily courtroom stress. Running simply saved my mind and provided clarity.

The lawsuit ended in a loss and an increase in our liability insurance. But the real loss is in some sense of humanity. You can do the right thing and still lose. Perspectives were changing. Michael was shifting from being a realist to a pessimist. I, being a natural optimist, was often just so frustrated with his views. For the first time in two decades since we fell in love, I started to be annoyed and irritated by him. He was sharing his thoughts with me and I was tuning him out. I felt like I needed a moment in a vacuum just to be with my thoughts, but there was no such luxury.

My sister and I got closer in this season; she knew our struggles and she was a safe place to make inappropriate jokes, an outlet to laugh. I shifted my attention to planning my 40th birthday. Let's have a party—it seemed like a good plan. My friend Cat put it all together beautifully. Fun times and distraction were welcomed. My first full marathon was scheduled for the weekend following the birthday party. I had the most memorable celebration.

Even though I enjoyed the party, I knew that moving forward, I would no longer be celebrating my birthdays with a party. I instead would enjoy a small dinner full of conversations—frankly, a sign of my new age. New experiences and adventures beat a party. A change in preferences is often a sign of new mental space. Take notes.

Shortly after the party and the race, I discovered I was being prepped for a new season in my life—possibly the most important part of my life thus far.

After the party, Michael seemed a bit distant. He was busy. He had split ways with his medical practice partner of many years. That lawsuit had left a sour taste in his mouth. We were fatigued as individuals and as a couple. We had been married for 13 years, madly in love for 21years. We thought there was nothing we couldn't overcome, I suppose.

Earlier in our relationship, while we were dating, it took days for us to talk about our differences. It was usually me, serving him a heavy dose of silent treatment. Michael hated when I did that. It was my juvenile way of serving a cruel and unusual punishment to him. As we progressed and matured in love and in life, we talked everything out. We had never had a "fight" in a traditional sense of the word. We always respectfully talked it out; what we are in public is what we are in private only better. So this season of just passing each other by, like a ship in the night, was unfamiliar to either of us. We must be experiencing a midlife crisis. Does he need a boat, a fast car, a mistress? We were both avid runners at this point; we had that in common. Kids are great; we had that in common. We love God; we had that in common—Michael is a natural-born scientist, church theory was losing its appeal. Sometimes, he would talk it out enough for me to know that there is conflict within him, on so many biblical topics.

"Why did God have to make Abraham put a knife in his kid's throat before He provided a ram?"

"Why did God have to impregnate a teenage girl to make a statement of salvation?"

"Who was Cain's wife?"

Valid observation, "Dear, just believe" was my usual response.

There was obvious conflict, growth and change in perspectives.

I took the time to reflect on myself, too. What do I need? I know I have to watch my sense of optimism because it is my greatest strength and also my greatest weakness. What am I protecting myself from? I am in love with my life, I think. I admire a lot of people, but there is no one I will trade places with in life. Fitness is an area I can stand to grow in. I loved running and after the big race, I fell back into yoga and I was enjoying the cross-training of yoga and running—not competing, just enjoying it all.

We were emotionally distant for a couple of months, just going through the motions of life. We were functioning well in life, but we both knew that our soul connection was not what we both have become accustomed to. There seemed to be a wall building between us.

We were having dinner one night after the kids were in bed. It was not unusual for him to be practicing medicine over the phone around the clock. The nurse on the other end of the call, on a speaker phone, was extra casual and was definitely crossing the line of professionalism. After he got off the call, I casually warned him to be careful—the nurse seemed flirtatious. I made a joke about nurses always trying to get into his pants, adding jokingly, that he was YBH—"young, black, and handsome." Stunned, he responded, "YES! You are right! I am struggling. The temptation is huge. I have never struggled like this." I looked at him, looking for the punchline. We often laughed at this kind of thing. It had always been funny how nurses threw themselves at him. But there was no trace of a smile. He looked at me like he was relieved to finally be able to tell me.

He was dead serious!! What? I was not expecting that! What? What happened? Have you crossed any lines? He had enjoyed being flirted with. What did this mean?

I looked up the literal word in the dictionary, since my face was burning with rage.

Flirting, as per my Google search, is behaving as though attracted to or trying to attract someone, but for amusement rather than with serious intentions.

I got angry. I was not even sure what I was angry about or why I was mad. I wasn't sure if my anger was justified. But I was mad. That was more than I could chew with dinner. I felt like my whole foundation was shaking from beneath me. Being married to this gorgeous man was a major highlight of my life. I stormed out of the dining room. I slammed the door behind me to my bedroom. It felt like a moment in some Spanish soap opera. He tried to come into the room. I had locked the door. I planned the rest of my life out—a dramatic moment for two tired souls.

I would have a plan in the morning, he would call his attorney and I would call mine. Were we divorcing? I was shaking. I wanted to go back out, hug him, and ask questions. I wanted to ask if he was okay. At the same time, I wanted to yell at him to rot in hell. How did crap hit the fan in just a very short time? Thankfully, the kids were upstairs. I stayed up all night planning out the worst-case scenarios.

I called my sister in the morning to fill her in. She said Michael already called her, asking for her help to calm me down. She talked some sense into my heightened state. She knows the two of us— Michael is the more logical one and I am the more emotional one. She reminded me of who I am, whose I am, and no matter what the details were, that I would be alright. But she also reminded me of who I married. "Michael is the epitome of a respectable and loving human. Professional beyond any other. He will put his life down for you and the kids. Can you just hear him out?" Overnight, Michael had called my sister, Audrey, and had updated and assured her, "There was no incident, just struggles!" My spirit said, "Chill," but I was everything but. My sister said, "Chill!" She knows I can be on the team "too much." She tells me the truth even when I don't want to hear it. "You literally married a man second only to Jesus; he adores you!" We were going through our first real trial. Distractions and stress are no joke; it had come between us. How would we move forward?

The next morning, the kids came down, we prayed, ate, and Michael drove them to school. We did our normal routine as per usual. As soon as the kids went to school, fear gripped me like never before. I did not want to interrupt this beautiful life. But I sure was not going to go along to get along. I was ready to fight my best friend to death if he had betrayed our family. On a world scale, this was not the end of the world, but for me, I was preparing for war! Michael came home from dropping the kids off at school. He had obviously been crying. He was sad that I was sad. I was mad as hell. But at the same time, I was crushed by his sadness. I gave him a letter I wrote overnight. I was so black and white and no gray. I let him know about our new arrangement: if there was any infidelity, he was to move to the guest room, keep life normal for the kids until we figured things out. He told me to slow down, that nothing happened. I would not hear any of it. All I wanted to protect was my own emotions. I did not want to live in some fool's paradise, better to protect myself than being left assed- out. My ego was the commander-in-chief. It was truly remarkable how quickly I prepped my mind to move it along. Was I to blame him for sharing that he is struggling? Was I supposed to give him grace? All the forces of life aligned. One thing was for sure in these dark days—I loved him! Even when I wished I did not, I loved him constantly! The world seemed dark! I felt alone. My ego would not let me speak up. We maintained our life—kids, running, work, church. My best friend called me out of the blue and said she had a dream about me and Michael. I told her we were struggling. She was full of faith and we have been through enough life together that this was not entertainment for her. She took it on. She shared some encouragement just as we both have shared with other people. My parents knew about our struggles and shared their stories to build my faith. My mom reminded me of my Grandma Grace and her story. "Every good marriage goes through this kind of season!" my mom said. And coming from 50-plus years of experience, I pressed pause and just sat in my darkness for a bit. I leaned into faith like never before. I stopped leading others in study, fitness, and school activities while I got my own spirit and mind right. I listened to a gazillion podcasts, YouTubes, sermons, and psychology. Every chance I had at work, I had on Les Brown and TD Jakes. I read their books. Not every voice spoke to my soul in every season, but I went deep into study after study. Solo. I was in this state for what seemed like forever, but it was only weeks. This is my marathon. I stayed in my mile 20 alone, digging deep, feeling faint but digging in deeper, getting closer to God. Keeping my heart soft and my skin thick, I took soul care to a whole new level.

I discovered layers and layers within myself. Ego is the real enemy. I had put myself on such a pedestal that I was not a safe space for my husband to even tell his truth without making him suffer for it. I hated to discover that I was a judgmental person. My soulmate expressed struggling and I did not extend a hand or a shoulder to lean on.

I went into a self-induced hiatus to explore my blind spots.

- What am I afraid of?
- What are my limiting beliefs?
- Why is my ego a factor?
- Is fear a factor? Fear of what?
- Am I a people pleaser?
- What motivates me?
- What drains me?
- Who drains me?
- What ignites my soul?
- Who ignites my soul?
- What do I tend to do when I am tired?
- Who do I admire? Why?
- What is my definition of a full life?

I have barely scratched the surface of who I am. It was time to tap into a deeper level within. That was the whole reason for these miserable weeks. To get my foot under me strong like a foundation that needed to be reinforced. Not parading through life in some kind of drama, but to live the life I was created for. Intentionally.

In the season of the lawsuit, lost friendship, and trouble in my marriage, it seemed like God's strategic plan was to get me alone to find out why He took the time to place me on this Earth at this moment in history. This revelation was stronger than ever to me. My kids were having some discipline issues, my sister was having troubles with her husband's immigration status, and our parents were having some health challenges. The emotional burnout was undeniable.

One morning in my daily devotion time, I had a divine encounter. I was directed to my own notes from a couple of years prior, in my own handwriting. I found the *Armor of God*, a study I led a group of women a couple of years prior written by Pricilla Shirer. I skimmed through my notes.

> "For we are not fighting flesh and blood enemies, but against evil rulers and authorities of the unseen world, against mighty powers in this dark world, and against evil spirits in the heavenly places" (Ephesians 6:12).

When I led this study, I remember naively telling the attendees that I do not believe that the devil has any power over anything. My limited understanding at the time said, I only acknowledge God and give no thoughts to the devil and its minions. I remember some women disagreed with me based on their own experiences. One passionate lady quoted John 10:10, "The devil comes to kill, steal, and destroy." I had a rebuttal for her, but God comes to give life, life abundantly.

The divine moment and how God brought the past to soothe my present and light up my future is that both are right. The devil and God are equally vying for my attention, spirit, mind, and body. It was simple but profound.

Ephesian 6:12 was lit up in my soul. Oh my goodness! I was at war!

My whole approach changed. You don't even have to be super-spiritual to see the playbook, even though I was going deep into super-spiritual mindset at this point. This fight was deeper than what was visible to the eye. This was the war of who I am now and who I am about to be. It was time to level up my mind and spirit.

1. My husband and I were going through a rough patch and complete burnout.
2. We were sued and drained.
3. The IRS was probing.
4. We had suffered the loss of our friends.
5. Medicare was probing.
6. My kid just spit in my tea.
7. My sister was in a stressful situation.
8. My parents were ailing.

I was in a fight for my soul, hope, and peace. The typical approach would have you pointing fingers at the things that have nothing to do about the thing. I had a new vantage point of view. The root of the posture of my heart was what needed attention. It was time to unplug and reset.

What was in me that was so great that the devil was at war to destroy all that I held dear? This was a holy time in my history. I would not waste this shift. No matter how it turned out, my mindset was now focused. It was a Friday, and I felt victorious. Nothing had changed, but my mind came out of the darkness and mentally I had a cape on. I was ready for battle.

I went to my closet. I wrote my thoughts down. I read the rest of the scripture. The words from the Bible do not leap out every day; sometimes it's theory. I have counseled so many people with this scripture. I have looked at other people's situations and applied the same verse from my own sweet spot, but on this day, my soul was muddled. It had been in a battle and I had been in a slumber, but on this day, my soul woke up.

What was my strategy? Now that I was wide awake and my spirit was strong, I had the feeling of being upside down after a quadruple shot of espresso. What was next? Should I go to therapy? I had never been to therapy, but I was not opposed to it. I assume therapy reveals 'aha' moments, which I happen to experience almost every week thanks to countless reading, podcasts, and studies I am constantly a part of. Suddenly, there was not an ounce of madness or sadness in my soul, just a thirst for what was next. How do I show up for myself moving forward? By faith. What was my next move?

Next verse, I calmed down. I recalled all the times I have led studies and coaching sessions. All the experiences shared by the ladies in the past literally flooded my mind. I have always marveled at what obstacles people are able to endure. The examples the ladies shared, I have coached them into the mindset that they need to have to be victorious. I was sowing and planting into my own future. I was helping them get through their nightmare when mine was not even a concept.

I was helping my future self. My future self would need the wisdom I was carrying around in theory.

Next verse please.

I soaked myself in reading scriptures more and more. The story of Paul and his commands of putting on armor for war to resist the enemy and win every battle came alive for me. I dove into the "belt of truth." What is my truth?

> "13. Therefore, put on every piece of God's armor so you will be able to resist the enemy in the time of evil. Then after the battle, you will still be standing firm.
>
> 14. Stand your ground, putting on the belt of truth and the body armor of God's righteousness.
>
> 15. For shoes, put on the peace that comes from the Good News so that you will be fully prepared.
>
> 16. In addition to all these, hold up the shield of faith to stop the fiery arrows of the devil.
>
> 17. Put on the Salvation as your helmet, and take the sword of the spirit, which is the word of God."

When the student is ready, the teacher shows up. I became a student everyday—intentionally looking to learn a new mindset. What was it that I didn't know? What was the mindset I needed to adapt? I devoted many predawn hours to self-development and growth. And I was never the same. I was no longer waging war on the people I loved. I positioned my heart up. It became personal. God, you can count on me. We have had a godly marriage for over a dozen years. We have never faked the way we love each other. As a matter of fact, marriage was the legacy we wanted to pass to our children. I have had friends pray for our kind of marriage. If we didn't pass this test, if we found an enemy in each other, that would be a loss for Team Greatness. That mindset brought me back to victory. However this ended, winning in everyday life would take the form of another letter of Paul. I devoured all the letters he wrote and published; the checklist of Galatians 5:22–23 helped me to go all out in living well.

> "22. But the Holy Spirit produces this kind of fruit in our lives: love, peace, patience, kindness, goodness, faithfulness, 23. Gentleness, and self-control. There is no law against these things!"

I went in deep on what brought the fruits to my soul. I was quiet. I was invited to lead a Bible study. I respectfully declined. I was being careful not to get too busy and abandon the growth I clearly needed to carry me into the next season of my life. This growth season gave me hope and expectation of a clearer perspective and a fuller life on the other side. Expectation is a beautiful way to wake up in the morning. The situations of life might still be the same, but with hope and expectation, my mind was open to lessons I would learn from my experiences of the new day. I paid attention to my emotions; I put them in check periodically. I must differentiate between my head and my heart. I found my daily prayers, meditations, and adding yoga back to my routine was anchoring me deeper into an incredible version of me. I felt a deep strength in my soul. Not the kind you see in the mirror, yet it felt like my soul had bulging biceps and triceps. I became extremely aware of when I am not doing what serves me well. Michael and I slowly but diligently worked on dissolving the walls built between us by stress and burnout. Michael found confidence in a good friend. Always great, when a good friend can say, "I have been there before!" He built his mind stronger, while I did the same for myself. Our love for each other deepened more than ever. We worked hard on being interdependent, rather than dependent. God was our common ground. What I noticed in this season was that I loved my husband too much. There is such a thing as that. I realized that being his wife was a source of pride for me almost in an obsessive way. I trained myself to walk back from putting my whole soul in him. The only space in my heart I should give without reservation should be reserved for God. It's the only self-preservation that makes sense. I got closer and bolder with God, made Him a nonnegotiable in my every thought, asking His opinion on everything, taking Him everywhere. What a powerful shift! I found a depth of badassery in this surrender. No announcement was made, but my confidence grew and my need to be paraded as a gorgeous wife diminished. I did not need to be validated by even the human I love the most. I had put my husband in the space that belonged to God. I put Michael in his place, second in command, releasing any stranglehold I had on him. It felt like a giant exhale. Life got more enjoyable for us.

I live my purpose; he will live his. We will always share our purpose, joyfully. There was so much freedom in that! I started to understand freedom of the mind on a new level. I was not dying to please any-one but always one audience, my Creator. Gosh, that's a really good feeling. The more I aim to please an audience of One, the more I find myself living selflessly and living my dream every day. What got me here is not going to keep me here, a phrase that always helps me to embrace change.

When an opportunity came to be a student in a freedom study, I was curious. For two hours a week, I met with about a dozen women. And the beauty of this season was that I was not a leader, I came in as a student. How you do anything is how you do everything. I went in deep. I took each word into action. My heart was opened for growth. It was as if God had planted me here at a time such as this. A couple of years ago, I would have probably been too arrogant spiritually to understand all the battles that people fight to overcome. My troubles were not to be disregarded because they was mine to overcome; at the same time, other people's troubles were theirs and not for me to judge. Frankly, most people are doing the best they can. I am a firm believer in continuing to study because a perspective change can change your whole life, suddenly. There's more freedom!

SOMETHING NEW

I took the freedom study alongside my bestie. She knows every step of my journey, struggles, and victory. She knows where all the bones are buried. We shared perspectives on our mountaintops, valleys deep, and every space in between. It is during freedom as I get more centered that I truly actually see the value in my own gifts. I have assumed that everyone had the same basic baseline in common sense and basic life skills. All egos aside, the more I talked to people, the more I came to the understanding that my parents were not just fluffing my ego. When they asked for my perspectives, they really needed the light I could shed on the situations. I had underplayed my own powers until now. My optimism and views of life when life got tough gave me the confidence in myself even more that the love and light I carry within me, which is not just for sunny days. The lessons that I learned in tough seasons were actually powers that made me think, "What else can I do?" Just sitting pretty in good times was not an option anymore. The purpose of my good times is to climb higher in the awareness of the possibilities of God in me.

I once read that, "You are either going into a hard time, in a hard time, or heading out of a hard time," which was all theory until after I was 40. The life that began at 40 is perhaps the more meaningful. I became grateful for everything and humbled by the grace to know better, do better, and serve others in more meaningful ways. The purpose of my optimistic worldview is to carry me and others by seeing the hope in every situation. I think back to my earlier years in the United States as a teenager and being evicted every month because rent was short and fees were added daily until it was paid in full by the 12th. I did not think that was hell, at the time—I was just grateful that I had a job I could double up on, to pay the next rent. That gratitude and optimism has helped to shape my thinking that no matter how bad it looks, I know it could be worse and that heart posture of "Gratitude and Optimism" is my superpower! The season of the freedom study helped me to acknowledge this simple fact about me. That is what I bring to every space I occupy. Boldly and joyfully, I bring me. In the past, I would fake or pretend doom, gloom, and complain just to fit in and blend in! When you know better, you have to do better. Bring your true self everywhere.

It was during the freedom study that I found the incredible next space I would climb into: yoga teacher training. The thought of it lit my soul on fire, not necessarily to teach but to create more awareness within my soul, a daily urge to my soul to live just for today.

What I learned from practicing yoga for a few years as a student is the awareness that this is the only moment I have to handle, just this one. Stepping on the yoga mat is a breath-by-breath step of what shows up. It does not matter the shape you have in your head; the only thing that matters is what shows up in this breath. The awareness to release the expectations of what should, could. The only thing that matters is now. The moment you look around to see what your neighbor is up to or how impressive you are, is the moment you fall flat on your face. Look up to be inspired by others in their lane of life, but it is important to keep all your energy in your own lane.

The root cause of bitterness and jealousy in most friendships or any kind of relationships is the longing to be in someone else's shoes. Stay in your own life intentionally!

Yoga training was a sweet 12-weekend commitment in the middle of my busy life. I eked out 200 hours out of a life that was incredibly busy, to remind me that I have power within me always to evolve and create my life adventures. My kids and hubby were proud and excited for my yoga-teacher-training season. They supported it to the end. Whatever comes next comes. I was not pushing. Winning for me was to have a whole new mindset. The cherry on top was sharing my mindset in teaching other people. It was not the physical teaching that excited me, but the transformation in mindset I got to share for 60 minutes—getting to share hope, love, peace, strength in the body, spirit, and mind. #Winning

BETTER ENDINGS

There is a unique destroyer I have observed as people of a certain age continue to encounter life slaying or being slayed by their giants. They throw the whole experience away because for one reason or the other, the experience turned sour at the end. Your experiences are yours to learn from—all parts of them. Learn from the good; learn from the bad. But forgetting to highlight the good and putting a spotlight on the bad will cause undeserved suffering. I notice this trend in marriages, parenting, businesses, and relationships of people of a certain age.

Think of the couple getting married—the light in their eyes, having enormous hope for the future. Fast-forward a few years, the same couple is divorcing, hating each other, sometimes literally coming for blood, battling for custody of children, and so on. Horrible things do happen; marriages end, relationships change, and contracts have to be terminated. Living in guilt and agony over the years for the bad part of the relationship while forgetting all the good parts is a disservice to self. Take the good part with you and replicate that in future experiences.

The more you love someone or something, the more you are apt to throw the baby out with the bath water to protect your heart.

I know two friends who have enjoyed partnership in friendship and business for decades. One business move caused a fallout. The partners will never speak to each other again. The good, the bad, and all the in-betweens were thrown away.

Highlight the days when the thing you have outgrown now was a blessing to keep ego from destroying decades' worth of memories.

The ending is even more important than the beginning.

Perhaps the most common case of throwing the baby out with the bath water is in religious experiences. This one is ongoing for me. The reality and ideal starts to be separate once you have lived for a bit. Born and raised in a religious household, religious rituals were a key memory of my youth. We only busted out the good china when the Catholic priests and bishop came to Sunday brunch. My mom will go all out and serve the best of the best. I got married in the Catholic Church, but my husband craved a more nondenominational gathering. We shopped around until we found the one we loved. Growth and great opportunities to develop great relationships were the selling point. The biblical teachings were ideal for our growing family. We became deeply rooted and loved every moment of it. Later, we noticed some hateful comments here and there, sometimes in undertones but soon in simple, plain, clear English. Take it or leave it. We chose to leave it. It no longer serves the purpose of building up our children and the values we hold dear to us and shared as a church for many years.

The temptation is to lump all churches together and put them in the "suck" category. So many people even go as far as to put God in this category and undermine the history of all that was good. All the bad preachers and mean-spirited pastors should not let you forgo the goodness of God and the relationship built along the way.

Throwing God the Creator away because you met a bad representation of him is irrational. The meanest comments in any media usually attach its rationale to prayers and faith.

Take the middleman out of the equation. Gather the list of all that was good, all that was learned, all the love. Throw away the demonic, manipulating, and controlling part. Learn the lessons, and enjoy the freedom of adding light to the beginning and the middle. Avoid horrific endings. How you end anything speaks of the nature of the soil of your heart. End well.

BETWEEN SUNSETS AND MOONLIGHTS

There is a unique perspective to life that comes from being born into a first world, yet spending all my formative teen years in a third world, and then my adult life in a first world. There is a feeling of standing outside of the situations of life and being able to navigate them differently. When you have seen so many layers of humanity in both worlds, it's hard to get sucked in, into a unidimensional point of view. This mindset is especially tricky as an African American, yet an African living in America. I notice I am less bothered by the forced image of whatever box the society wished to put me in. For better or for worse, I take myself mentally out of the grouping that doesn't serve me well, for instance, the stereotypes "Africans are so loud" or "African Americans are so lazy." I instantly refuse to absorb it and cope by grasping a deeper understanding of myself, "I am not going to fit a narrative based on some limited beliefs of African or African American." This type of coping mechanism saved my mind beyond my twenties. Mentally belonging to no group and being okay with being an outsider, I found people with like minds to be in my tribe. I was smart enough to know that I needed a tribe. I have trained myself to look for the friendly mind in any space I am in and build a tribe that expands my mind.

My tribe as a teen was a small group of gig teens who would stay up all night studying at the local Country Kitchen, knowing darn well they have an 8:00 a.m. class and work at 2:00 p.m. An unusual bunch of all races, mostly second-generation immigrants, sat together and dreamt of a future they had never seen in their lineage, but were naïve enough to know that a high GPA was all they needed. We were literally bulletproof to any ideas that were designed to kill the spirit. My accent was thicker than steak, but I just cut right through it and repeated my words as many times as it would take for my peers or professors to digest it.

The audacity to be young and bold. Dear 17-year-old self, walking and speaking boldly in a continent that is new to me, I can only imagine the heaviness of my Nigerian accent. The coping mechanisms of what I term as a second world. Even today in my forties, I find myself sitting comfortably in my lane observing and differentiating between the worlds. I live in the fastest growing city in the United States. And my second-world mind is always on the go. I find my first-world friends' mindset at work with what I will define as "vanity" such as the perfect nose jobs and skin pulled back, or the need to have the newest edition of anything for the next season while the current one is in perfectly perfect condition. Nothing wrong with the excellence of beauty and near perfection, but obsessive chasing of "me" can be draining for most. The desire to keep on being on top, being the best, and being the most liked is so consuming. That must be what the good book meant by "the love of money is the root of all evil."

On the contrary to that is the "just get by" mentality of a third world: if it isn't broken, why bother to fix it? And now I observe third-world mentality in first-world locals and vice versa. Neither mindset is optimal. Balance.

I am constantly on the search for the perfect balance, a sweet spot where you care enough but are not obsessive. Not seeking everyone's approval but enough to get you motivated and inspired about life and what's next in your journey. The balance is a bigger struggle with the invention of social media.

On my recent trip to Lagos, Nigeria, it was a Saturday morning. It had rained and the air was crisp and the grounds muddy. The cool temperatures were a welcome relief to all. The comfort reminded me of my kids back in Texas. Do they even appreciate the basic privilege of electricity, tarred roads, air conditioning, and abundance of toiletries?

My mom and I decided to take a long walk around the neighborhood while we enjoyed each other's company and the beautiful cool morning. It is safe to say the neighborhood was full of working middle class. About half an hour into our long walk, at the end of the community were a group of teen boys playing soccer. I am a die-hard soccer mom—all four of my kids play soccer, I am a huge fan of watching them, and my husband is a straight-up fanatic player and watcher of the game. As I got closer to the boys playing soccer, I stopped to watch. They were loud, happy, joyful boys just playing around. But my attention was more focused on the conditions. Fast running, intense competition, and only one boy had shoes on. There were no soccer cleats, fancy socks, or uniforms—just skills on skills on skills. As soon as they saw me watching, they upped their tricks. Showing off and in that Lagos slang, they were saying, look at me, I got more skills. I was fully entertained for close to half an hour. I was most impressed and overwhelmed with the joy. The joy they felt to be playing; teeth-showing joy! Undebatable joy! I could not help but compare the attitude in Lagos and in Texas where I usually spend my weekend days at soccer fields.

In Texas, the fields are green, uniforms are world class, and cleats run in the hundreds of dollars. Water bottles are uniquely designed with engraved initials. Spring and fall soccer were simply the best. Parents on the sidelines cheering, snacks are labeled—but where is this kind of joy I just found in Lagos? The teeth-showing joy! Lucky-to-be-here-playing-soccer joy! Often after a game, I find myself asking my children, "Why the long face?" To which they will respond, "I am tired. I just played a game." The undebatable joy cannot be taught. It's a mindset. The only way I can describe it is privileged and entitled. Both are necessary mindsets that require balancing to thrive anywhere in the first or third world.

IF IT COMES, LET IT; IF IT GOES, LET IT

That is the single lesson God and the entire universe has been trying to get into the depth of my being for a real spiritual awakening. The scenarios are all different, but the overall lessons that set me free are simply "let it go," simple enough but gosh the impossible level of maturity that is needed to execute. And in almost any difficult situation I face, 99 percent of the time, the solution is, "Self, let it go!"

Let the pettiness go.

Let the expectation go.

Let the disappointment go.

Let the friendship go.

Let the business go.

This is perhaps the hardest lesson to learn, yet the most liberating when put into action. The idea of not forcing anything is what makes getting older a more peaceful place—a place where you can truly see a value in your intentions even when the external forces do not approve. This skill would have saved my sanity a few years ago when I was in complete despair over what I was certain was a misunderstanding. I spent many sleepless nights trying to amend partnerships that had lost their magnet. It took me many seasons to be able to look at myself in the mirror and release the magnetic force. Not all things or partnerships are meant to last forever.

Don't force anything. A few years ago, an opportunity for a partnership came to my husband—the opportunity to travel the world and practice medicine in poor and remote parts of the world. He would be doing great work for humanity while he enjoyed life. This could be a life mission to continue forever. We started with the organization. It felt especially in tune because I came up with the name of the organization after my morning devotional one day while we were vacationing on the beautiful Smoky Mountains of Tennessee. For sure, it was divine; God was all in it. We were so excited. Our friends, soon to be partners, got super-excited and moved ahead with all the legal portions of the organization. And before we could all wrap our minds around the "what, how, who," the ball was in motion for the organization. Things were moving quickly and we trusted our friends/partners to tell us what the next sequence of actions were. Websites were started; staff was hired. We kept asking questions for what we needed to do now that the ball was in motion and we were newbies in the not-for-profit world. There was an awkward silence. We got suspicious because the level of excitement the partners shared was now nonexistent. We were being edged out; an email went out to all the boards. An email was sent out and we were clearly excluded. I took it personally. It was not until a few weeks later that another friend was bragging about how awesome "our" organization was that I looked up the link and found out, indeed, we were not in the loop to this great mission.

Naturally, I was filled with emotions I could not identify. I attempted to call a dinner meeting to talk it over or at least know the reasons behind the decisions to exclude us as a couple! Our friends would not meet. They tossed us away like old salad. I wish I could get over things in a moment. Disappointment with people we know and trust hits the heart differently. I was tormented for a while. I needed to know why they disapproved of us. Our history together made it very personal. Did we have a blind spot? Did we do something awful? Was it something I said? My extroverted self must have hurt someone's feelings. I tormented myself hard. My ego was in my way. The experience put a spotlight on my need to please people. I worked on finding balance in how I deal with people and their opinions of me.

Some of the advantages of maturity that came for me mostly after 40 are to know that your style of life will not be appealing to everyone. So much time is wasted forcing into spaces that are not shaped for us and using all our energy to squeeze into them. If you dim or brighten your light to join the masses, someone will still find it lacking their preferred shade. Find where you are celebrated and shine your light naturally.

Who knew Elsa said a lot when she belted out the song "Let it go!"

My yoga teacher training taught me, "Life is a fine dance of balance of holding on and letting go!" This principle might as well be the 12th commandment. It's a tool that allows one to just live in the moment, in whatever way the moment presents itself—not in a reckless living kind of way, but in an adaptable mindset to evaluate how things are, and honor the moment. It requires checking in with the soul and having a conscious awareness of releasing the "old" that does not serve you well no matter how much you crave the old and going deeply into the "new" and how it presents itself.

Elevate your soul to searching more space of freedom within.

Practice balancing holding on and letting go.

In relationships that end, balance the beautiful memories and let go of the possibility of what could have been.

The same principle goes for romantic relationships or marriages. There is a fine art of balancing the memories of all the good times and letting go of whatever caused the demise of a relationship. I believe this is why some exes can be in each other's life in a healthy way. Not letting go plants a giant tree of bitterness and a lifetime of war within the soul and everyone around is a casualty of war.

Children are especially vulnerable to being targeted when the grip is held tight on the past rather than the possibilities of the future.

Relationships, feelings, and dreams come in seasons. Letting go of the old only releases space for what and who is to come.

Someone once told me an analogy of a great traveler who came back from a trip. He collected his bags from the airport baggage claim. He had his hands full. His two little daughters excitedly met him at the airport baggage claim. They ran into his arms, but he held on to his baggage. He did not quite get the hugs and affection his children were showing because he was holding his bags. The only way to enjoy the goodness coming your way is to literally make a decision to let go of the baggage that you are holding on to.

In various seasons in any relationship, you have to intentionally let go of what was not optimal in the past to enjoy what is now, or what could be.

In marriage, we ideally share every part of our lives. In various seasons, one or both will go through changes. Expect it. Always be changing and looking for changes in your lover.

Mentality, mindset, or midlife: You want your spouse to evolve, knowing that not all changes are welcomed. Sometimes you need time to process the change. Once we were all packed up ready to go on our wedding anniversary trip; I believe it was well into our teen year anniversary. Hubby casually mentioned, "I wish you would wear bold eye shadow colors." What? He casually expressed like the ones on the *Housewives of Atlanta*. (In my mind, those looks are trash.) My idea of a great trip was casual, no heavy makeup. I asked for honesty, but I didn't necessarily like what I heard. Hubby was wishing for a goddess look, and it was stress inducing to me. Love me in all my wretched ways all the time! Damn it!

It took me two of the four days of vacation to literally intentionally release the baggage of what I interpreted as a rude comment to me. But then, against my ego, I decided to not ruin my own experience and dressed up more than I desired with the decision to play with more makeup on that trip.

Releasing the grip on my ego that tells me a story to stay offended despite Hubby's repeated apologies for the way I heard his request. I chose to enjoy the much-needed couple time and embrace the fact that what got us here will not keep us here. I intentionally grabbed my own face in the mirror and told myself to let it go. There is room to enjoy new experiences.

When the mood was lighter and I had no need to be so defensive, we had a conversation about the eye shadow saga. Was it really about the eye shadow or something else entirely? There is wisdom in knowing there is always a root cause to every conversation. He was going through a change of mind, taste, and being. How could he tell me what he likes as a spouse without me taking it personally as a personal insult? Sugar coating is good, but on the long haul, deliver your truth. Till death do us part is a long time to the miserable. We took advantage of the open hearts and defenseless atmosphere to explore new ways of blowing each other's minds in and out of the bedroom.

Where do you have some growing up to do? Ego check is a form of self-care. Surprise yourself by opening up your mind to new ideas. Get your ego out of the way and embrace the possibility that change is good. Stagnation causes staleness. Keep ideas flowing. Change often.

Water is refreshing and life giving unless it is stagnant; then mold and algae grows on and in it. Be like water; keep flowing. Ideas in; ideas out. Flush out old ways of thinking, being, and doing often and create a vibration of new even in the same story.

The change we need frequently need not be drastic, but continuous and consistent. Tend to the garden of what you care about and continually till the soil to reveal the beauty of the next season. Attend to what you committed to. Attend to your spouse, business, children, family, and organization. Hold on to continual evolution and continual letting go.

Releasing the person you have always been, find strength in being open and find deeper strength in what could be. The work of evolution is not to make a grand announcement to the world that you are changing. The announcement is to yourself, in your own soul. When you find yourself getting angry again and again in the same situation, make a declaration with yourself to breathe through and hold on to your power within rather than losing your temper at the same things. That is how you personalize your growth. Let old ideas, offenses, insults, and attitudes die while new space is developing for the new. Choose to change the most important thing—your mindset.

Living in America in 2020 showcased the racism that has been an issue for decades. Naturally, only the people affected were deeply torched by it. After a series of documented murders of blacks—cases like George Floyd, Ahmaud Arbery, Breonna Taylor, Daunte Wright, and on and on—and so many attacks on people of Asian descent based on the frustration and finger-pointing concerning the COVID-19 virus, I realized that there would be no change to the overall mindset of the population. The change I needed to focus on was my own mindset, to bring the change I wished to see in humanity to everywhere I go. Waiting on the world to change its mind was draining all my energy out.

"Let things go!" Not just a little bit, but 100 percent all the time. Love all the way!! What if it falls apart? Then I will deal with the disintegration when it happens! Then, I will dig deeper to go through all the pain required for the process of letting it go, but make that a goal. Yes, it's hard. Sometimes holding a grudge may seem sweeter, but overall health of mind and full life requires a healthy dose of "let it go."

I married into a loving family. I lucked out in the in-law department. For many years, it was smooth sailing. But when we got to year

15 or so, my mother-in-law went through a season where she was not a fan of mine. She let me know it, too. There was a decision to be made. Retaliation or choose to be the peacemaker; either way, my spouse would be the recipient of whatever I chose. I chose peace. Peace was not bowing down and being insulted; peace was simply not to engage—not to respond to what was for sure meant to be an insult. I simply engaged less; I removed myself from the situations that required conversations, at least one on one for a while. As per my nature, retaliation would probably feel better. Confrontation would be kind of fun—for the moment. But there are fights you choose to remove yourself from especially with people who mean something to you. Retaliation would hurt my spouse, the family dynamic, my kids' grandparents.

It was not long until my "Peace agenda" started to be effective. It was a very short season of conflict. I didn't even go back to discuss her mindset or motive at the time of conflict. Once she became her sweet, caring self again, we were back in a relationship. And the only kind of relationship I choose to be a part of after 40 is the kind that mirrors how I am to myself, kind and nourishing 100 percent. I completely let the rough season go; no residuals.

Let it go!

10,000 HOURS

Research has shown that it takes 10,000 hours of practice to become an expert at any field. Apparently being a prodigy with a "gawd given" talent is just a myth. Only one who devotes himself to a cause with her whole strength and soul can be a true master. For this reason, mastery demands all of a person. 10,000 hours works out to be around 20 hours per week for 10 years.

I remember when I was a first-time mom to be. I read all the books. I did hours and hours of research and asked everyone I knew about their experiences. What do I need to know? I bought two copies of *What to Expect When You're Expecting*—one for me and the other for my husband. I dedicated a lot of time to learning before the baby's arrival—from the birthing process to holding the baby to the entire first year. It was nothing like I had expected. What I knew in theory did not apply. I had to experience it. I had to get a feel for my baby and respect her preferences, habits, and mannerisms. It was dedicated hours day and night. All the research was not a waste of time. They were necessary to build some foundation, but the real work had to be done with great care and attention to every turn and cry. There was no substitute for the work.

By the time baby number 2 arrived, 17 months later (by the way, breastfeeding is not birth control, but I digress), I had a better handle on newborn care. The new expert training is how to be a parent to multiple kids. Caring for the toddler and the newborn was another opportunity to master a new chapter in parenting.

The more hours you put into whatever field you choose, the more of an expert you become. You build confidence in it until it becomes second nature. There will be new challenges along the way, but embracing the change and adapting to the new innovations keeps the growth going. When you acquire new skills, use them.

In December of 2018, I got certified as a yoga teacher. I was so proud and excited, but also scared out of my mind. Yoga has been so therapeutic for me and I looked forward to sharing that with others. I accepted a teaching position in January of 2019. The early morning has always been when I am most creative and vibrant, so I chose to teach the 5:00 a.m. class. The excitement and the nervousness I felt for the first class and the first few months were beyond believable. I did not sleep a wink all night thinking of the sequence, music, my accent, my body, and my students. I will write everything down and change it again and again. My 10,000 hours began the first day I taught. The training leading to this moment was just theory on being a teacher. The first hour was when I started teaching. The worries were different. Will anyone show up? Will they like my style? It would take at least 100 hours before I started to enjoy the journey and relax my shoulders, breathe, and enjoy the views as I adjusted my style on my way to 10,000 hours, learning new lessons along the way. That is why it's practice. The same applies to medicine. Medical school and residency training are foundational. The real road to being an expert in your field begins when you are done with training. Hour one is when you are face to face with your patient and there is no sounding board. I remember Michael had books from different sources to back up his treatment plans and diagnosis right after residency. He read all the new and up-to-date journals in medicine. Fast-forward to two decades of practice—he is now an expert in the practice of Internal Medicine. Rarely do strange cases show up in his daily patient care.

Stay diligent and vigilant because being an expert in any field, if you are not attentive, can lead to being complacent. Stay open to new ideas and the cutting edge to incorporate changes into any art that you have mastered. Add new training or certification to keep the excitement in your field.

Place yourself in rooms where you are the novice often. This is as equally important as getting to be an expert in your field either personally or professionally. Put yourself in a room where you are a complete "idiot"—a room where you look around and you are the bottom of the totem pole. Ask all the questions. Get new perspectives to a new or old idea. Demolish the comfort zone trap. Be a beginner in something often. Don't hold your curiosity in; at the risk of appearing stupid, ask all the questions. Update your mental software as often as you can. Don't let your ego trap you into believing you have arrived. Stay curious at the opportunity of learning.

I watched my husband agonize when he was studying Economics. A seasoned medical doctor was feeling like a newbie in a finance class. The comfortable zone is where dreams go to die. Put yourself in the uncomfortable spaces often. Grow and repeat.

PANDEMIC 2.0 RACE TO SANITY

I tend to put my words down on paper more often when I am in uncomfortable head space. The desire to write eludes when I am happy and skipping along with joy. I barely go to my journal when I am in a happy season. I write a lazy "Thank You" when I am feeling joyful. But when troubles arise in my world or in the world, I become Maya Angelou, prolific writer to clear my mind—therapy.

I feel the weight of the world heavy on my shoulders as I see my kids getting taller and seeing the injustice that is randomly directed to people who look like them. It did not hit me as hard as a young woman probably because of my dual citizenship and my formative years being in a part of the world where everyone was of the same race.

The death of Ahmaud Arbery, an unarmed young black jogger in Georgia, hit home more than usual. The truth is with every publication of racism or police brutality, I get more and more overwhelmed. When I was younger, it was a distant wahala, a huge trouble over there and not here. I have told myself a false confidence—that I am educated, in a certain tax bracket, and so forth—all lies I have told myself to be able to cope with life. But as I catch a glimpse of my children's image as they pass the room, I get more fearful. My son is a young black man who runs in the neighborhood just like Arbery. Can this happen to him? We are in Texas. There are still some confederate flags being flown on some trucks as we drive by. Can we be safe? As a mother who has sheltered the minds of her children from the reality of the black experience strictly to keep their minds powerful, there is a huge conflict. Teach and expose them to all the reality and injustice of black lives, or keep them believing that hard work and great attitudes can get them to their highest calling. The sadness is overwhelming. I noticed that most people still view blacks as a fraction of a whole human. Not by words but by actions- a built-in bias. When the student is ready, I guess the teacher shows up.

I have always been so aware of my need for organized religion. I was born and raised Catholic. I was married in the Catholic Church and that was at the top of my identity until my husband begged me a couple of years into our marriage to consider an alternative so he wouldn't die of boredom. He asked what principles I would like for our, at the time, "unborn kids" to abide by. We landed in a nondenominational church. We loved it for many years. Being active and serving at church became my passion. Being a part of a community and culture fed my soul. I got to lead women in studies and was actively able to serve with my children in teaching other children.

When my dad died in February of 2020, and was buried in Nigeria, more than a dozen priests flew in or drove from afar just to be a part of the final respect. I am a student in the classroom of religion. I started to examine my motives.

What is it that I need from my religious experience? I believe firmly in God and I find a unique peace when I communicate with God in a daily study. As life will have it, COVID-19 shut all churches down. My Sundays became devoted to personal Bible study, yoga, and listening to sermons and podcasts as I cleaned my house or sorted the laundry. The more time I had to listen, the more I saw the politics in church. The more I paid attention, the more tension rose within me about collaboration of church and politics. The more I dug, the sicker I got!! Was this whole fiasco of western church a game to the powers that be? I was reminded of the churches above the slave grounds in Africa and all over the south of the United States.

By the time George Floyd's public execution by way of the knee on the neck happened in May of 2020—more than 9 minutes of begging for his life—my heart left my body for many days!! How could this be happening in this day and age? I got fearful for my kids' future. Can they be safe? My teens just got their driver's licenses. They were planning for their futures and deciding on colleges.

My pastor said, "We need not rush to conclusions. We need more evidence!" What? What more evidence do we need for centuries of evil displayed differently? I somehow thought we as humans could see evil and call it what it was. I desperately wanted to believe that.

I had to come to the realization for myself, "Why did I expect a different response from another human?" I was so deeply troubled that my religious community did not have a heart for what I had a heart for. I felt a betrayal to simple humanity.

I realized I placed weight on the opinions of religious leaders. I felt a hole in my heart for just another human expressing his opinion that I saw as ignorance. It would not have bothered me as much if the opinions were not from the pulpit. It's a reflection of the state of my heart and I did not like what was revealed to me.

I was holding other people to a higher standard I wished on them. My expectations were placed heavily on all people doing/saying the right things. I was finding my hope and stability in the "man of God." I needed this lesson more than ever before. I showed up intentionally as a student to everything ever since my dad's burial. I prayed that all my blind spots were exposed. I wanted to have real perspectives, not manufactured or fake ones to get me through life. I wanted all the blinders removed. Online church afforded me the luxury of listening more and allowed me to stop being so distracted with doing. I listened intently to all the "leaders" and their tone. And I realized, sadly, that most are influenced by politics, by the heaviest tithers, by the culture, and very little to do with the immovable word of God. My foundation was all shook up. I had not been paying attention. I shared my heart with my sister. She apparently was not surprised. How can you have no diversity in leadership in your church where you have been taking your children for 15 years and not see that "your point of view does not matter"? My mind immediately flashed back to conversations with a lot of friends who had sought out diverse leadership for the sake of their children. Yet it felt like I was hearing it for the first time. This further shed light on the state of the human mind: You only hear what you want to hear. You hear what supports your way of thinking. I was so hopeful for the world that I wished for that I put blinders on to ignore everything that did not support it. Love is truly blind.

The moment the video of George Floyd's murder was not met with empathy and heartbreak by every human of every race was when I realized how demonic the human soul can get. Demonic has no limit, from the pulpit to the streets. My teenage daughter was surprised by my surprise to the church's response to the wicked murder of George Floyd. She had been studying history and noticed the correlation of the past and the present. "We might stay home from church," to which she casually responded, "I am surprised you are just now making that decision." She said she had been waiting for me to become aware of the lack of inclusiveness of church. No one who looked like her held the microphone or provided leadership. She was just waiting to go to college to find her own vibe. I was astonished. I asked her why she had not brought her concerns to my attention. She said, "You would not see it if I told you. No black girls in the Christmas story, Easter story, etc.; love is blind!"

I have always tried to be honest with myself. At this phase of life, I know I have not told myself the truth about reality. I wished for a better world, so I bypassed every idea that did not support my wishes and just jumped into my idea of reality. The more I read up on history, the more I realized I might be a part of the unconscious bias tribe, unconsciously biased to love and equality, unconsciously biased to justice for all. Even though the facts support injustice and equality, I am such an optimist that I looked the other way. I made up reasons why this would not happen to me, my zip code, my well-behaved smart kids, or my culture. I was so naïve, it was bordering up with ignorance. I felt stupid, hurt, and angry. I have tied myself down with religion and made-up stories to protect my mind and to keep my neighbors comfortable.

2020 was a year of clarity—a year to bust the bubble of the façade and the lies. Blindness is a condition you can accept and learn to live with! Once your sight is restored, there are new responsibilities that cannot be accepted as is. Expectation even to self is great once vision is restored; denying the sight and pretending to go back to blindness is simply not an acceptable "truth." Thinking the same way but expecting different outcomes is simply insane. Know better, think better.

WALK AWAY PEACEFULLY.

Maturity looks different in every season. Sometimes speaking your mind is maturity; other times, simply walking away is maturity. Not waiting to give or receive explanations is a different variation of self-preservation. Perspectives in faith, race issues, and politics is a slippery road to engage in. But in 2020, they all collided. These are the hardest things; we have two options. Engage and get wisdom from each other and possibly growth. Or the easy way out, say nothing and let things continue in our world status quo!

The only way to preserve the confidence and dignity of my four young black children is to find a balance between the reality of life and the big dreams I have for them. Humor is a way to teach the truth while keeping the spirit light. And, frankly, I find it an effective means to deal with a tense reality. I often ask my teenage son to load the dishwasher or some other chore he despises, and he will jokingly say, "Oh, because I am black?" "Yes, because you are black! Get in this kitchen and give me your best effort."

The responsibility to keep the kids' minds sane is more important to me than the loyalty to one side of the story in the world than the other. The important thing is to be able to see facts and make decisions based on that. The system is rigged to favor some over others, but hard work works. Most people have been conditioned to be biased about one race over another. These are facts. Always see the facts and make rational decisions from facts, not emotions. Know when there is bias against you. Know when to fight it; know when to save your energy for what is right. THINK FOR YOURSELF! Even if I was white from the Netherlands, I would still look at the facts, at the history, and come to the simple, human, basic civil conclusion, "Black lives matter!" And God forbid there is an attack on any group of people that I am not a part of, I will want to take pride in humanity and shout out, THEIR LIVES MATTER!

My neighbors on the side of privilege say, "Look at me; I matter! Don't forget about ME!" They think, "All lives matter" during a race crisis? I am looking at you; I see you. I see your ego, arrogance, and uninformed status. Equality should be a nonthreat to anyone! Supremacy or suppression should be a concern to all people of any level of sanity. The more I read up on history, the more I applaud Black Americans for seeking out equality, not revenge. Bravo Negros.

SHAKY GROUNDS; SHALLOW RELIGION!

Every now and then I go back to the red letters of the Bible and refresh my memories on what the lesson or the point of a parable is. What was Jesus talking about? It's refreshing the perspectives the words take based on the level of my maturity and mindset; my interpretations and lessons vary. I recently was having a conversation with a good friend who is turned off by all things religious based. There is a thing to be said about the interruption to the normal pace of life in 2020. The interruption caused a pause in the normal rhythm of our thinking. It seemed like before the 2020 pandemic, life was a rat race, or rather a hamster wheel just moving and doing without much thoughtfulness attached. Parents were too busy to teach. Christians were too busy to be Christ-like. On and on we went, being busy 24/7 without really feeling a sense of accomplishment or being effective.

The series of unfortunate events—aka 2020—came to help us to refocus, to redefine our minds. It was time to calm our spirits, to capture our thoughts, to get our egos in check, to check all the labels and make necessary adjustments. Are you a hypocrite? Are you bound by the opinions of others? 2020 came to break the chains we camouflaged. For goodness' sake, it looks like we are all being played. Leadership is out for its own good, even at the expense of public health. I used to pride myself at seeing the logic behind others' thinking; the bizarre thing of this era is the irrational behind the thinking pattern. Even more confusing are the people who label themselves as people of faith and a specific religion that engages in meanness and bullying tactics that are the exact opposite of that label! Yet these people believe to the death that they are right and everyone else is wrong.

During the 2020 pandemic, after I taught a yoga class on a beautiful Sunday morning, one thing led to another, and before I knew it, I was knee-deep in a conversation about race, politics, and religion initiated by one of my students (a rookie mistake). Frankly, I avoid having such conversations with people outside of my immediate family because I understand that so much emotion can be aroused from any or all of those topics. I will call him Mike for the sake of illustration. Mike was a good sport and the conversation was quite informative. He is a white man; I, a black woman. Our lenses are different. He is a great human; I know that. He was respectful, so I figured this would be a safe space to explore the mindset of a fairly conservative White Evangelical during the 2020 pandemic.

I asked, "Tell me, what is your reason for not wearing a mask to possibly curb the coronavirus?" He looked at me like I was being ridiculous. He gave me a Bible verse about the possibility of the Antichrist and that he is covered by faith. I told him that the statistical and factual data supports that wearing a mask in close spaces could help curb the virus. He came back with, "The media is fake, and the numbers are inflated." I was relentless; I came back with my reality that is not media driven. My husband is a practicing physician and his COVID patients have tripled, with sicker and younger victims. He shrugged it to happenstance.

We jumped into race issues. Here, I was determined to listen, really listen. He, too, was of course saddened by George Floyd's execution but said that the Black Lives Matter organization was a sham and demonic. How about black-on-black crimes and murders? he parried. I agreed that that was an issue, but the system is unkind and makes the cycle of poverty continue in these neighborhoods. He agreed.

Lastly, and the most impactful of all, he asked me, "How could a supposed Christian like yourself not support Trump's policies 100 percent no matter his level of meanness, aggression, and discriminating tone?" Mike said that the more the media is against Trump, the more he is for the 45th U.S. president frankly because it was Christian versus the world. At this point, I understood what I had been confused about.

The 45th president gives comfort to the population of Americans who believe they are losing something. He seemed to be the one who could restore whatever they feel was lost. Since that conversation, I pulled back on my emotional investment on current issues knowing that there is nothing I can do to change other people's belief systems, but I must protect my sanity by just letting people do what's good for them and I do what's good for me. I will be vocal with my views, fight for what I believe in, and leave the rest. That freed me. The fight of Christians against "the others" was not my fight. Frankly, the more I see a Christian in the fight, filled with venom, the more I distance myself from the label. It was getting downright dangerous for the world.

I went back to the red letters of Jesus and read them repeatedly. I fell in love again with His words. He already predicted this chaos. All those parables were for today. I can trust Him. When he said, "Above all, love" was the greatest and most important thing, he knew that was going to be the hardest thing. The New living translation of the Gospel of Matthew records "Jesus's replied, "You must love the Lord your God with all your heart, all your soul and all your mind. This is the greatest commandment. A second is equally important: "Love your neighbor as yourself." (22:37–39). When I was younger, it was a piece of cake. The older I get, the more I guard my heart and my neighbors are getting harder to love. There is even a parable for that. He said the workers who have been working all day will get bitter toward the end of their day because of fatigue, comparisons, and expertise. Be laser focused on guarding your heart. The organized religion that saved your soul might also turn it into a cage. There is freedom in love—loving yourself and loving others.

Mike continued to get more and more aggressive with his defense for his faith and views on pro-Trump beliefs. In January, he drove 1,600 miles to the Capitol to be a part of the Insurrection of January 6, 2021.

Everyone finds a chapter and verse to defend their actions. How do we know that what we are doing is right? I need simplicity. Where is the moral compass? Again, I went back to an anchor that I can trust in Galatians 5:22–23.

"22 But the fruit of the Spirit is love, joy, peace, patience, kindness, goodness, faithfulness, 23 gentleness, self-control; against such things there is no law."

OK. I can support that. Simple enough for me to digest and plant deeply into my children. I have been researching to find my blind spots. What am I to learn here? What is my religion? Was I blind then, or am I blind now? I see clearly, but have I seen clearly before? My mind is formed, but how do I help my littles to form a mind that loves God, their Creator, and enjoys his creations? Above all, love, but don't be stupid. See the bias against you or your kind, but rise above it. Always use the compass above to guide your next steps. The storm of 2020 did not come to destroy. It came to awaken all our senses. No more lying to self. Wake up. Look in the mirror and decide who you want to be. The golden rule is a lifesaver if we can be disciplined enough to apply it.

"DO onto others, as you want them to DO unto you."

Use fruits of the spirit compass:

- Is it Lovely?
- Does it bring Joy?
- Is it Peaceful?
- Are you Patient?
- Is it Kind?
- Does it serve goodness to humanity?
- Are you being faithful?
- Are you being gentle?
- Are you practicing self-control?

Say "Yes" to all of these questions and that is worth investing your energy in.

The study of human behavior has been such a fascination of mine, but 2020 provided nothing but pure fascination in the ways of human reasoning. I constantly find myself asking others, "How can you support that thought process?"

The major events of 2020 alone—no matter what your views are—give a preview to the human mind and how it holds on to whatever it chooses to believe with or without evidence to support it. A narrative is created in the mind and evidence is sought out in the world through all means necessary to support it—the level of offenses and certainty held on to by the proponents and opponents of any issues, the degree of anger and resentment thrown unto those who we find as opponents in belief systems, the levels of certainty that the "others" are idiots and we are right is a deep exposure of our maturity levels.

Move forward; hindsight is 2020.

This is a safe bet even in the world where everyone has turned up the level of their own certainty. There is no better time to self-evaluate than now when the axis of our beliefs and norms are shifted.

The epitome of intensity is what 2020 has shown us, from the worldwide COVID-19 pandemic, to worldwide protest of "Black Lives Matter," to the tumultuous presidential election in the United States, to the siege on the Capitol in 2021, and what seems like endlessness in brutality of humans toward each other. The level of offenses based on political stance, racial preferences, and faith wars are unmatched. It's healthy to check the soul for any roots of bitterness that were planted in any way. I find some unintended bitterness raging within me towards the system and towards humanity. I realize the way of the future must be to uproot the daily deposits of bitterness and develop a mindset that will fully enjoy my existence, accepting what is and doing my part with what could be while maintaining a sense of true optimism in humanity. The future begins with me, and it begins now.

BRANCHES

Sticking to the physical representation of a tree in the analogy of the life journey. The branches transports materials from the tree trunk to the leaves. The way to a vibrant future is branching out and explore the possibilities in our range of being human. I follow an older lady on social media she is in her late seventies and living a life full of confidence and joy, often in a bikini and exploring new adventures. She shared the secret to her vibrancy as exploring all the areas of her personalities that she had tucked away once society deemed her too old, motherly or too successful to be a certain way. I see this virtue in my own Mom, she is constantly finding new ways to live an exciting live. Exploring new ways to add joy to the moment and the kind of vibrancy to be reminded by. Exploring deeper and exposing brightly and boldly is the currency to the future.

DUALITY: WAY OF THE FUTURE.

The Merriam-webster describes duality as a noun.

/Du.al.i.ty/
 : the quality or state of having two different or opposite parts or elements; a dualism.

The kind of future that the world demands from us is different. The mindset that served our parents will definitely need to be switched up to enter the age with the next generations of thinkers. Just like the first series of Apple devices needed an upgrade to its software to be useful in the future. If the initial generation of devices had not been upgraded, the device could make a phone call, but with an upgrade, it could be a library of books, a window to the world, an entire office.

The same kind of upgrade must be done to the mind, often and always to stay relevant and knowledgeable. One of my favorite quotes was written by Paul and it poses a challenge to readers to constantly renew—and some translations even call for a daily transformation of the mind.

> Romans 12:2 "Do not conform to the pattern of this world but be transformed by the renewing of your mind. Then you will be able to test and approve what God's will is—his good, pleasing and perfect will."

If you don't look back at your journals, pictures, or decisions of the past and cringe at the way your mind was and how far you have come along in the journey of your mind, may I challenge you to the challenge of "daily renewal and transformation"? There should always be a transformation going on in the mind as long as you are alive. Your values can stay the same, but your extension of love and expression of your values always has room for transformation.

The pull to stay the same can be appealing, even comforting, because the more you live, the more skin you have in the game of life and the more you have to lose. Your tribe will want you to stay loyal to your old mind to keep the boat from rocking. But the journey to embrace change opens more effective windows of the mind and lets more light in. Pat Robertson, media mogul, televangelist, political commentator, and former Republican presidential candidate, advocates a conservative Christian ideology and is known for his past activities in Republican Party politics. He has made hundreds of millions on his predictable views and has had a loyal following for decades. It was not until his 90th year that he started to have a transformation of his views. His proponents and opponents in views were stunned by both the negative and positive ends of his arguments. It's never too late to release the hold your own mind has on you. Consider new perspectives as you grow in life experiences. A mind is a terrible thing to waste.

There is more room within. Explore.

CHANGE AND STAY THE SAME

Embracing change and keeping a sense of self are not mutually exclusive. Both mindsets can exist in the same space. Being grounded and truthful to self, while embracing the changes around and within, is growth. There is power to not be in the box assigned to you by society. Someone once said they are surprised by how I vote! The point is to embrace a new way of thinking. Staying the same is a waste of all the experiences that we have gone through. When I was younger, I was, without any exception, pro-life. The older I get and educate myself, my personal stance stays the same, but my opinion on others and legislation on the matter has shifted. Everyone must hold on to the power of their choice. That is not compromising my values, but being open and respectful of others in their own journey. My own mom made a choice that she still deeply feels decades later. There are enough self-imposed consequences; there is no need for others to add guilt and shame to the life of others. I once participated in a life study and the leader broke down at the secrets her parents forced her to keep and the pregnancy she got rid of as a teenager. That was the first time she spoke of it in 30 years, even though she cried at the anniversary yearly. Self-condemnation met with righteousness and judgment of others leads to bondage.

Judging others is a burden and it feels like a huge favor to read the Gospel with a new pair of eyes that releases and commands us to "judge not, so we will not be judged." Whew! What a gift that is!! It is the freedom to put my whole nose in my own business. That is as close to the gift of salvation as they come! But, this was a gift I did not use in my youth. Growing up Catholic and backed up by two generations of Catholics, we walked proud in our righteousness. Often the conversations that provoked the most excitement were the "sins" of others. I remember how women in my family would grin and chat forever about the hell that awaited any person in the community who had left her husband for another. I remember my parents feeling sorry for one of my beloved Aunts, because she is not worthy of the "holy communion" based on who she married. My mom would grin and tell the story of how she only had eyes for my Dad; I knew she felt closer to God because of her "right-ness." A few years ago, a public figure's daughter had an affair with a family friend, which caused the end of both marriages. I could hardly wait to get home to tell my husband about the scandal. Once I laid it all down, I expected him to jump on the "right-ness" of us. He expressed deep sadness for the situation. I did not want his sadness; I wanted us to rebuke the perpetrators and feel good in our obedience and goodness. He said this would be entertaining if it were not reality and painful for the parties involved. At that moment, I knew I had a lot of growing up to do. There is a generational mindset of comparison to feel better about self. I had not noticed until that moment how much I based my values and pats on my back on the downfall of the minions around me. It was time to embrace change. I worked on reprogramming my thought process. I planted my standard deeper in an anchor that never fails. I am no better or no worse because of the situations of people around me. I became less "church-y," more empathetic, more joyful for other people's successes, and less boastful for the reason to make others shrink. It's a whole new perspective to the world by just shifting a mindset. What else can I learn? Learn from any and every situation. You don't know what you don't know. I recently allowed myself to watch the documentary on the dog-fighting incidents of Michael Vick. Michael Vick was a NFL quarterback who was accused of cruelty to animals and sentenced to close to 2 years in prison. No doubt what he did was horrible. He paid his debt to society. He was reformed and continued to find his way. What I observed were the commentaries of others. An analyst recommended an extreme death by execution for Vick's crimes in 2010 and stood by his decisions. Fast-forward to 2020, the same analyst justifies the death of George Floyd by the knee. Most talking heads stay the same publicly because they have worked hard to create an audience. Choosing to embrace the ideas of others—be it media, politicians, or religious leaders—rather than sitting in your own thoughts and finding the truth out for yourself by using your own senses and consciousness numbs the ability to tap into the power within. There is a whole market paid to tell you how to think and gets you fired up on what to think and keep you there. Stretch your mind. Dare to embrace the thoughts between your own ears, explore the possibilities and perspectives. Explore what you believe deep down to your core and not what is fed to you by others.

There is a time to be fed some milk and there is time to grab the steak knife and feed yourself.

CONFIDENCE AND SELF-DOUBT

Confidence is a feeling of self-assurance arising from one's appreciation of one's own abilities or qualities. Self-doubt is lack of confidence in oneself and one's abilities.

Can confidence and self-doubt coexist, in the same space at the same time?

Yes. I believe they balance each other out. I am a confident person with self-doubts on so many abilities until I have strategies in place to be confident in those abilities. Waiting to be confident in an ability will not happen until time has been spent practicing it. Start with shaking and trembling, know that the process of self-doubt is the building blocks to building confidence. What is empowering is hearing the stories of the greats and how doubtful they were of their abilities. The same ability that I admire them for is the same one they diminished because it seemed unimportant to them in the grand scheme of things. The common self-check and self-doubt of "Am I good enough?" is necessary to keep working on the skills that will make you feel confident. Then, find a new inability, doubt your abilities, acquire the skills necessary, fail loudly in the process to build confidence, and repeat over and over until death. Stand in your confidence and notice the doubt. Let the confidence speak louder than the doubts. The doubts are the catalyst to keep you up at night to push you to refine your craft. All the "greats" feel the doubts and do it anyways. I was astonished at the revelation of Michelle Obama, when she expressed a lot of self-doubts even as she operated as the first lady of the United States of America. Do it shaking; just do it. Constantly work on something that puts a fear of God into you. When I was 10, my mom went back to school to get her Masters in Accounting. She moved into the dorm and we visited her on the weekends. I saw her struggling with the balance of various examinations, making new friends, and juggling us, her family. It brought excitement into the thought of my own future. Up until then, I assumed a woman picked her career, chose her husband, had kids, and worked till retirement. The idea of evolving and changing brought freedom and excitement into my future. And now when I discuss the future with my children, I let them dream in plurals. Have several seasons of your choosing. Learn continuously and overcome self-doubts at one level to gain confidence into the next level. It's a whole lifetime of level ups. Once you have mastered a level, keep your mind open for growth and grow accordingly; otherwise, what seemed like growth can end up feeling like a trap if you stay stagnant for too long. The job you get and throw a party about can become a trap if you don't keep seeking a new level of growth. The same goes for people; keep exploring your friends, loved ones, community, and yourself to find the nuggets. You are good enough and deserve all the levels of greatness! The level of doubt that goes into writing this book even with the insane knowledge that what I have to say is valuable even to one. Confidence and self-doubt both have internal volume knobs.

Some days the volume of confidence is high and drowns out the self-doubt; some days, it is vice versa and the volume of self-doubt makes you want to shelve all your hopes and dreams. The sweet spot is to find the balance and find the factors that turn up the volume of confidence and turn down the volume on self-doubt. My level of confidence is deafening in the early mornings before dawn. I have spent some time meditating, journaling my gratitude, and acknowledging the awesome gift of life. I get creative in the mornings believing I have been placed into this day to be effective and strategic in how I spend my day. I work with great effectiveness and see the plans into the future with clarity. I am most kind in the mornings. I adore my children in the mornings. I make them the best lunches, recite positive affirmations, and look at my husband in honest admiration. I turn up to a new level of great confidence after a midmorning workout. The juices really flow and I am simply unstoppable.

Any time after 7:00 p.m. is when the volume of self-doubt is deafening for me. I am tired, spent, and I look at the children with a side-eye. Dinner, if not planned ahead, is chaos. I am not the best human at dusk. I doubt my ability into tomorrow. I am overwhelmed by the responsibilities of raising and feeding children and my husband—it's best to just leave me alone. My office feels like a trap and I look at the outside world with envy.

Observe your patterns and capitalize on them. I front-load my day and get important things done. I am constantly working on how to make my evenings more enjoyable, but I know I cannot trust the fatigue and the self-doubt of my mind in the evenings; I practice my affirmations more in the evening to remind myself of the greatness within. The evenings are when I make phone calls to the people I love. It nourishes me to call my friend, my sister and really enjoy a girlish conversation in the evenings. It boosts the volume of confidence for me.

Confidence is fresh and new every morning. Turn up your confidence volume. The doubt volume is not going to be muted because a little doubt helps you to sharpen your skills and hold you accountable to yourself, but the level must stay under control.

COURAGE AND FEAR

1928 Merriam-webster defines both dualities of courage and fear-

Courage: mental or moral strength to venture, persevere, and withstand danger, fear, or difficulty.

Fear: an unpleasant emotion caused by the belief that someone or something is dangerous, likely to cause pain, or a threat.

Fear must be present at the same time and in the same space for courage to come alive. There is no universal value to courage other than moving forward in the presence of fear. What is fearful for everyone is different; therefore, the levels and kind of courage needed are unique.

The first time my middle child, EmiGrace, went to the beach as a 4-year-old little girl, she literally curled up in a ball and cried when we asked her to play in the waters. She felt safe at the shore, building sandcastles. The ocean seemed like a giant monster to her. Her older siblings have always loved to just ride the waves, over and over. It took enormous courage for EmiGrace to just dip her toes in the water. She was intensely stressed, but we kept returning to the water and making her face her fears of the ocean. Repetition and reinforcement helped her jump in by the fifth day. Her siblings thought it was ridiculous to be afraid of the waves. Different fears for different folks. Honor the limitations of others and present a safe atmosphere to face them. My son surfs the waves repeatedly, but was once terrified of public speaking. Any presentation project at his IB curriculum school was like a hammer to the skull; he was painfully shy. Every time he stood in front of the class and presented his work, he was facing a mountain of fear. He would imagine all the eyeballs on him as naked people sitting on the toilet. His fears slowly dissipated as his courage increased. Naked people in the middle of a bowel movement presented a safe space to present his works with just enough courage.

Building courage is an individual endeavor. After my dad died and we were at the funeral, it was time for us kids to give a vote of thanks; my brother and sister would rather eat paint than speak publicly. They required courage to speak up; I needed no courage, speaking in public was no fear for me. Writing for me requires no courage—it is therapeutic actually—choosing to publish takes courage. The fear of my ideas being rejected is what I need courage to face. I have been working on my fear of pleasing people for a few years. I admire people who did not give any care to what others think. It's a process for me. Every year, I notice it requires less and less courage for me to fully show up as my authentic self, knowing that I will not be openly received by all, but I still show up. Courage is the one character trait that I admire and wish to grow more in always. I notice shots of adrenaline into my veins when I notice fear and intentionally pour courage into myself.

Being a power yoga teacher has been a lesson in courage.

What if the students hate a class you have carefully prepared? The lesson of "Take nothing personally" has saved me from internalizing other people's reasoning. There are times that I had to cancel because no one showed up, and there are times it was a full house. Either way, keep learning and striving to be your best and face the acceptance or rejection with grace. There is never a loss, only learning opportunities.

Learn. Privately and publicly. Face your fears no matter how trivial or magnanimous. There is a whole different experience of freedom at the other side of fear. Be strong and of great courage was repeated more than a dozen times in the Bible. For example, Deuteronomy 31:6 says, "Be strong and of good courage, do not fear nor be afraid of them; for the LORD your God, He is the One who goes with you. He will not leave you nor forsake you." "Fear not" is mentioned 365 times in the good book. Expect fear, find your fears, and, more importantly, find the courage to face them. Do one thing a day that is courageous. Saying hello as you pass a stranger by might be courageous if you are afraid of being ignored or rejected. Reaching out for help is a form of courage when you stand the risk of being ridiculed. Attending an exercise class can be courageous if you fear looking weak or silly.

Find your fears and create an unstoppable list in your mind of ways to be courageous. Your courage is yours; once you find courage, more confidence is within reach. It is a muscle that gets stronger with frequent use. Flex your courage. Waiting for the perfect time will delay the inevitable. Just do it. Fail loudly and learn. One of my favorite TED Talk presenters, Luvvie Ajayi, presented the topic "Get comfortable about being uncomfortable." An excellent talk, Luvvie was flawless, confident, and informative, but in an interview, she revealed how sweaty and afraid she was moments leading into her presentation and how she did not feel confident until she was half-way into the 10-minute talk. Many notable greats share the feelings of overwhelming fear and finding exhilarating joy and confidence when the fear is faced. Jesus was scared out of His mind at the approach of His crucifixion. He begged to be released from the obligation of death. However, He faced it with courage. Most of what scares us will probably not end in life-or-death consequences even though it might feel like it.

Most of what we fear will never happen. I have a litany of fears of losing my loved ones to death or tragedy. I have observed and counseled people who have suffered sudden loss. The courage to overcome any situation is available within. When a friend suddenly lost her husband to a heart attack while on a business trip overseas, I was paralyzed in fear for her. She found strength within to move on and raise their children with joy. Five years later, she is thriving over the heartache and pain.

As a young mom, I was fearful of dying and leaving my children without care. This was a strong fear until my friend Gina was diagnosed with an aggressive form of breast cancer. We watched her as she slowly succumbed to the horrible disease. She left a daughter who was only seven years old, the age of my older daughter at the time. I was devastated and questioned the mercy of God. Her husband Tom wept like a baby for months. But he kept showing up with courage for their daughter. A couple of years later, he found a beautiful young woman to love and joy was restored in a different, unplanned kind of way. I have seen couples who are insanely in love end their relationships and they survived the heartache by facing it with enormous amounts of courage. Perhaps the most courageous and life-changing moment for me was when I was having lunch with a friend and she asked at the last minute to bring another friend to lunch. We were introduced to each other and exchanged pleasantries, she kept talking about her child. When I asked how old her child was, she casually expressed losing her 5-year-old to leukemia, about a year prior. She had a twinkle in her eyes when she honestly expressed that she couldn't believe she was chosen to be her son's mom and beamed at how having him for five years was the greatest honor of her life. In that moment, with tears in my eyes, I expressed my condolences for her loss. She left a huge expression of courage in my heart. There is no need to live in a hypothetical state of fear. There is always power to tap into courage when and if needed.

The yogi in me takes one long, slow breath and then decides on the simplest step forward to the great unknown into the next breath.

There is no way around fear; feel it, face it, beat it. Repeat.

AUTHENTIC AND YOLO

The Merriam-webster dictionary describes authentic as an adjective.

/Au·then·tic/
:true to one's own personality, spirit or character.

There is a duality of living in truth and living in the moment. Both are needed in the same space and at the same time in the same person. Finding the balance adds a dose of excitement into our routine. We live in the #YOLO era—you only live once (expressing the view that one should make the most of the present moment without worrying about the future, and often used as a rationale for impulsive or reckless behavior).

There is a pull to show the world that we are successful right here and right now. The motive to show off to ourselves and others has been revolutionized by the invention of social media. From simple things to great decisions, most of the motivation for a #yolo lifestyle is magnified by our need to be seen. Last Easter, I found myself shopping for the perfect Instagram-worthy dress. I did not know if my family would attend any events or what activities we would be a part of, nor what we would eat to celebrate the yearly celebration. I zoned out on all of the details, but I did desire a great picture for my album and to share with the world. My misplaced priorities were displayed right in my face on Easter morning when my family did not care to pose or go along with my shenanigans. They wanted to just enjoy family time with no announcement of it to the world. I respected their wish. Later on in the day as they were hunting for eggs, hiding and seeking, wearing play clothes of their own choosing, and with random dog toys scattered everywhere, they asked me to take their picture. Oh joy! I jumped at the opportunity. How many times has the desire to be seen crowded out the need to live in the moment? Bringing this duality into our immediate consciousness is a tool I am adding into my future as a necessity. The media age is here to stay. We influence each other in this era by what and how we share. Your next vacation spot, next workout, outfit for the day, and so forth are influenced by what other people allow us to see or are sometimes paid to share. The image shared is perfectly edited to appeal to our senses.

I sometimes record parts of my workouts to share on Instagram with the intention to inspire someone else to get off the couch and move. I am not sharing the angle where my stomach is hanging down to gravity. I show the angle that flatters my body. It's the highlight of the workouts. When I dare share the unflattering angle, even my husband calls me out, when my highlights have all the rolls of skin. I am a mother of four via C-section; my #authentic and #yolo intersect when I work out. The not-so-perfect angle will be the inspiration for some and the turnoff for others. You must accept the facts that you are not for everyone. Your message in person and online will not be for all people. Accepting that you are not for all people will free you from defending every disagreement of ideas or following of friends. Bending to the whims of others to please will shift you from showing up as your authentic self and, frankly, it is exhausting to show up other than your true self. If Jesus and Chocolate have critics, you too must give yourself freedom to be who you are right now—authentically. Your critics will live or not. #yolo

On a bigger scale, the conflict of #authenticity and #yolo can cause a great divide. Planning a vacation, wedding, or party that will be wowed by others even though your pocketbook says otherwise can be very detrimental to your relationships and your pocketbook. There are times that you throw caution to the wind and just live. Even those times, too, have to be thought out and calculated to weigh the value of the #yolo event to the consequences. Consequences will remind you to sit your tail down and remember you are too cute for jail, your children are watching, or you will be homeless if you move forward.

A young lady of Nigerian origin I once mentored graduated from a very reputable med school and finished her residency with brilliance. I will call her Kathy for the sole intention of learning from her experience. She got offered a job as a senior partner in her field and quickly became a leader in her field. She was invited to speak in her community as a health advocate. Her life was ideal and attractive from all angles. The only burden she felt was that she was 35 years old and single. Her parents were adding pressure, "Your eggs are rotting." At first it was casual and then the intensity grew the busier she got. A family friend introduced her to a suitable young man to date. It was not love at first sight. There was no chemistry between them. Kathy was a hard worker and her suitor was a casual entrepreneur that had no solid plan for the future. They kept trying to create chemistry between them. When the guy moved to the same city Kathy lived in and seemed to be pushing for more intimacy, Kathy went along with putting more effort into their relationship. She introduced him to her family within a couple of months. Her Nigerian parents started to plan a wedding. The extended family overseas were so excited, they started to apply for a visa to travel for the wedding. When the visas got approved for more than two dozen relatives to travel from Lagos to Texas. It was a done deal. There was no outlet for Kathy to back out or express her doubts for the union. The planning commenced. The invites stationaries were royal. The asoebi aka the family and friends uniform attire was announced. It was beautiful and expensive. The wedding locations were top of the line. Kathy expressed her concerns to her mother, "You will learn to love him, all the tickets have been purchased, we will not want to shame the family, would we?" Kathy knew she had no love for the dude but she got to a point in the process that she just picked the #yolo mindset, she saw the joy the wedding planning was giving her family and there was not space to turn around. She turned up her vibration and spent more than $100,000 for the most lavish and colorful Nigerian wedding I had ever seen. Wow indeed. I was really rooting for Kathy to find the magic in her new husband. The marriage lasted a very short 100 days. There was no love or excitement that magically showed up after the wedding. The marriage did not even pass the honeymoon phase.

When the choice is between authenticity and #yolo. Think it through. There is adrenaline flowing in the yolo phase but you will have to live through the consequences of the aftermath. Evaluate the prize. Proceed accordingly.

Some #yolo moments are not done to impress others but to satisfy a craving by simply enjoying the moment. It might look like a great time to flirt or have a quickie with someone other than the one you are with. Sure the pool boy, or the young sexy lady, or whoever looks really good and is temptation for a great time outside of your committed relationship, but will the action to follow through on your impulse ruin your life forever? Think it through. You can have an enjoyable, spicy life without bringing doom into your forever. Find a way to merge your #yolo and #authentic life together to create your own unique kind of magic.

A friend went to a company Christmas party a few years ago. She had a few drinks beyond her limit. She found herself in bed upstairs at the hotel with two of her coworkers, in a ménage à trois. Probably a #yolo moment, but the moment led to loss of her executive position and a nasty divorce.

Either for show or for your own satisfaction, explore the ways to balance and merge your #yolo to your #authentic reality. I have observed too many people suffer the consequences of not balancing the authentic and yolo impulses. Impulses can be planned to create continuous magical personal or professional events. The balance comes from defining what is important or the desired outcome ahead. Center back to your authenticity. Who are you? What is important to you? Write them down. See them in black and white. Written-down values cannot be swayed by emotions and impulses. There are not enough words to express the importance of written-down values and goals. Placing written words where they can be read often, preferably daily, will help be a reminder when impulses and the need to impress screams to take over.

If college savings for the kids are a priority for you, write it down. Place a reasonable timeline to it. Emotions and impulses shift; values written down on paper stay unmoved by circumstances. If you don't have a value that anchors you, your boat drifts everywhere.

A ski trip to Aspen with friends is going to look like a #yolo event you cannot pass up at the expense of college savings. Write your goals and values down. Make it plain. When your authentic life is the life you are living, there will rarely be a need to keep up appearances. No need to keep up with what you said to whom and where. You just show up and your "yes" is true and your "no" is just as true. No mask on. Your business persona should be in alignment with your casual persona. There is no energy wasted in parading as a person you are not. The real you is the best you. Show up as is, even as you work on a better version in one area or the other. The real authentic you has no fear of missing out #fomo- Fear of Missing Out. You can embrace being the life of the party or a tired mom who needs to be in bed by

8:00 p.m. People often want to identify with you based on how they met you. That is not your obligation. Show up as you are based on who you are today, in this setting, in this mood. Tomorrow will be a different feel; that feel will be analyzed when we get to tomorrow. I can be dual and it is not opposing. It aligns with my core values. It might look like opposing factors to the world, but it's true to you. There is no need to justify your core values to the world. But you must justify them to yourself.

KIND AND BADASS

The next duality going into the future will really get you out of your box. Whatever label you or the world has put you in probably requires you to be the same person, think the same, and allow no deviation based on your mood or season. For many seasons, I contained myself to fit into a bite size that is easily digestible by the world. It was not until my 40th year that I gave myself the permission to adopt the courage to seek a larger version of me that I always suppress.

Being kind is and has always been in my DNA. I feel a sense of satisfaction by being kind. /Kind.ness/ is the quality of being friendly, generous, and considerate.

I am that. No doubt. I display that part of me proudly. It is a godly trait and I am proud of it. But also in this vessel is a badass. I did not embrace this version of me until later in life. The more I live, the more I want to expose this hidden treasure.

/Bad.ass/ is a tough, uncompromising person. The older I get, the more being a badass feels like a godly trait. The journey of badassery is only possible when you drop the weight of caring so much of other people's opinions. You laser focus like an eye of a tiger on the outcome that you desire, long-term or short-term. Training for a marathon was my first acknowledgement of this trait. I had to dig deeper to find a reason that is beyond my norm. The "why" at first was to be impressive, but once I started digging deeper, I realized that I had to be tougher and intimidating to my current self to get to the future self that will be able to finish the task at hand. Kind was not going to cut it. I had to tap into borrowed badassery in my music, podcast, author, and friendships. I read the book *Can't Hurt Me* by David Goggins over and over again. I read up on the greats that I love. What kind of badassery is required for Tina to survive Ike? What kind of badassery is required for Beyoncé to survive the initial scandals of Destiny's Child or Becky with the good hair? There is a mindset that is needed when crap hits the fan. I want that mindset along with the mind I already have and appreciate. Embrace duality.

My newfound partnership and friendship was with Shon. She started out as my running coach, then we became accountability partners, and soon we were on full blast beast mode. My initial assessment of Shon was that she was not looking to be liked. She once told another runner to kick rocks, right in front of everyone. "I will never do that, I am too kind," was my interpretation of the moment. Later over lunch, as I discussed with Shon to call the girl back and apologize for her "meanness," she looked at me like I had horns, "No ma'am." The end. She later said, I only have meaningful relationships, no fluffs. No false apologies. What?? Shon lived in my head rent-free for a whole week after that conversation. I loved the authenticity in this godly and badass woman. I admired her freedom to be true to her emotions. I chose to adopt that mindset at least in my running goals. No BS. I started to pay attention to what I wanted to do and carefully deliberate on doing them. Merge my kindness to my badassery. It was and continues to be a winning combination for me. It helps me to tap into my own unique powers. It started out small, like running in my sports bra. I had been wishing to do that but somehow I had convinced myself that a "normal mom" should not do that, even when that's all I wanted to do. It was a splash of badass to my mindset. I parade this belly that has housed four humans like a badass. Sometimes it's a six-pack abs and sometimes it is a soft PMS belly. I show up with kindness to myself as a complete badass. This duality of kind and bad to the bone is what allows me to take on a new challenge like a boss. If I fail,

I show kindness to myself; if it works out as planned, I gain a level of confidence and advance to the next level. I don't play video games, but if I was a gamer, this would be the admittance to the next level. The higher my badassery, the higher my level of trusting my own thinking. In July of 2015, at the height of summer heat in Texas, Shon and I ran over 200 miles in those 31 days as we prided ourselves all around the trails and sidewalks in our medium-sized town in our sports bras. We were exchanging character traits and building strategies for our various futures. Shon was mastering kindness; I was mastering badassery. There is so much value in both. I have used faith, maturity, and motherhood to suppress my badassery and Shon had a litany of events that almost canceled her kindness. There is space for both to drive our everyday career, fitness, and family life. What is badass looks different for everyone. Find yours and embrace it.

Me writing this for you to read is one of my badass moves. As long as I am alive, I will keep finding new ways to do uncomfortable things that will be my price of admission to the next level of thinking. This will be valid as long as there is breath in my body.

The most valuable role model was Jesus as a human. He wept when His friend Lazarus died. He was so heartbroken by His friend's death. And fast-forward to another day: He got so mad at the traders in the temple, He literally flipped the table. "Jesus made a whip from some ropes and chased them all out of the Temple. He drove out the sheep and cattle, scattered the money changers' coins over the floor, and turned over their tables. Then, going over to the people who sold doves, he told them, 'Get these things out of here. Stop turning my Father's house into a marketplace!'" (John 2:15–16)

Allowance to tap into more/different from within is the most powerful tool as we mature. The tendency is to stick to the same way we have always been. Don't. There is more within as long as we are alive. Keep searching for your edge—your new edge. It is new daily. Find it. Enjoy it. Live it.

Kind is great, but I am more than that. Every now and then, be a badass.

LEAD AND FOLLOW

The Dead Sea is the lowest point on Earth. It is more than 1,400 feet below sea level. The water is 10 times saltier than any other bodies of water. There is no outflow of the Dead Sea; it is not conducive for any kind of life. In order to stay fresh, water has to keep flowing. Stagnant water smells. The picture of a waterfall is powerful. Getting its source from a larger body of water and flowing to smaller bodies of water, creating energy in the direction of flow. The analogy of a waterfall is worth adopting into the flow of our lives as humans. You are water in a waterfall. Keep being fed from a larger force or body and keep feeding into a smaller body. Keep flowing—continuously—in every aspect of life, spirit, mind, and body. There is no need to reinvent the wheel. Only God the Creator of the world does not need a mentor. Find a place in all areas of your life and find mentors to pour into you. It does not even have to be in person. You can be mentored by a podcast, a book, or an autobiography. Place yourself in a room where you are receiving knowledge, wisdom, and information, a room where you are open to ask questions. Let all your guards down and just be a student. Equally important is finding yourself in a room where you pour into others. In this room, you are the source, the light, and you hold nothing back. You teach what you know honestly knowing that you bring a unique perspective and experience to the world. It becomes a give-and-take kind of world. Know that the more you give, the more space you will create to receive.

As a young parent, I find parents of older kids who are thriving to learn from. I pick the brains of my own parents on how to raise my own children. I stay curious on what's important to remember and why they made the choices they made, what the hardest obstacles and triumphs to expect and at what age—it might not be applicable to my case, but I stay on the lookout.

The waterfall of wisdom and experience lives by continuous flow. Receive with the intention to give. Most people live with the scarcity mentality believing that teaching or telling from their wealth of knowledge will limit their opportunities; the Dead Sea mentality is not conducive for growth and life.

As a yogi, I stay open to new experiences. When I was a new teacher, I attended every yoga practice as a teacher, constantly taking notes and adopting a new language and knowledge of alignment and anatomy of the body. With experience, I learn that I must step on my yoga mat with intention of how I receive or give a class. Am I a student or teacher here? Once I gave myself the permission to not always be learning and accumulating, I found myself as a better student. I turned off my ego and simply enjoyed my practice—shoulders relaxed, jaws unclenched, and long and deep breaths. In return, as a yoga teacher, I started to enjoy teaching even better—pouring what was poured into me knowing that my voice is not anyone's voice and that is my superpower.

The fluidity to lead and follow has no boundaries. Be open to be a leader and a follower within moments of each other. Yoga has been a teacher of many useful lessons to me—the mindfulness of being aware of what parts of you are needed in the moment. I had been looking forward to taking Deb's class all week. She was one of my yoga teacher training coaches. Her class always leaves me exhilarated and yearning for more. Every opportunity I get to take her power vinyasa flow, I do. We have been building a slow friendship over the years. On a particular Thursday, she was particularly spectacular, paying attention to every cue and moving in every direction of that 24X68 magical yoga mat, the gentleness and the intensity of the flow at the same time. I felt like I was at mile 1, 18, and the finish line of a full marathon race at the same time. The class was only 60 minutes long. I always feel like a new teacher after Deb's class. As per usual, I went in to give her a hug for a spectacular job she had done and what a teacher she was. To my surprise, Deb looked at me with sadness, close to tears and expressed that her mom was in the hospital overseas and she was worried sick. Immediate role switch: my teacher needs a teacher. I grabbed her hands and assured her. I led a prayer of peace to invite a greater God into the situation. Her mother will be well we agreed as we shared love, light, and exchanged sweaty hugs.

The same applies in business, marriage, friendships, community, or wherever we find ourselves. Be a river, not a reservoir, in every aspect of your life.

Lead and follow, teach and be taught.

HUMILITY, EGO, AND PRIDE

Probably the most important duality in life and especially as we acquire experiences, wealth, and expertise in the journey of life is the balancing act of pride and humility, and a third wheel that is attached to our subconscious, ego.

Pride, according to Webster's dictionary, is a feeling of deep pleasure or satisfaction derived from one's own achievements, the achievements of those with whom one is closely associated, or from qualities or possessions that are widely admired.

Humility has a dictionary definition of a modest or low view of one's own importance; humbleness.

Ego is a person's sense of self-esteem or self-importance.

Just by definition alone, pride looks healthy and attractive to me. I literally send my kids to school with a bunch of affirmations. "Be proud and enjoy the satisfaction of your efforts" is what I tell LillyanJoy, my second grader as she proudly tells me of her 25/25 in less than 2 minutes in her subtraction math facts. I have never encouraged my kids to have a low view of their own importance. I have been instilling pride and not humility. Why is pride considered a negative character trait and humility embraced?

Pride is the first of the seven deadly sins: pride, envy, anger, lust, greed, gluttony, and sloth are called the "deadly" sins because they are biblically the chiefs from which all other sins spring. Pride is the exaltation of "self" above all authority, even God's authority. Pride is cosmic arrogance.

This midlife clarity of duality is one that I find is in my every thought process.

How does pride become a deadly sin? How is humility a godly trait? How can I recognize and balance out the pride and humility? After reading *Ego Is the Enemy* by Ryan Holiday, I became aware of the role of ego in the human psyche, the weight or emphasis that I put on self. Upon reflection, I observe that ego is the key to balancing pride and humility.

The law of relativity is not only applicable in physics. The difference between the pride that will help you reach your goals and the pride that turns to a number-one deadly sin is relativity.

- Are you comparing your deep pleasure to others?
- Who are you comparing your accomplishments to?
- Are you open to correction?
- Are you critical toward others?

This can be as simple as a second grader beaming with pride for a job well done on a subtraction test. Suppose the same child now gets so much satisfaction from her work that she thinks there is no need for her teacher and looks down on the other kids who are challenged in their learning process. The child, if not corrected, will continue to attach the degree of her success to the level of failure around her. On and on to the state of not wanting to be corrected or taught new ideas because she believes she knows it all. Watch the arrogance in yourself and how you view yourself.

Check your ego is not just a cliché. Literally gather yourself and the space between your ears and what shows up in the different phases and aspects. Check your ego in every room you enter. This mindful exercise of simply checking yourself is as honest as you will ever get.

What is my heart posture here? Stay open and mindful to where you are humble and prideful. Be able to analyze yourself without judgment. Just observe.

You can be:

- A proud CEO and a humble parent
- A proud doctor and a humble patient

- A proud cross-fitter and a humble runner
- A proud giver and a humble receiver
- A proud software developer and a humble real estate developer

The duality of you. Notice you. Keep studying you because change is inevitable. Your humility and pride will also change. Check your ego often. There is a fine line between being proud and satisfied of your achievements. Check your gauge and heart posture to ensure that you are not living in the #1 deadly sin realm. You can walk and chew gum. Balance.

Consider the relativity of you and God. Even if you are an atheist, you have to know you are not supreme. There is a creator who puts all the elements in place even as the scientists prove creation right or wrong. You don't know all there is to know, even if you devote your life to studying; you are not the supreme.

In the same breath, you are competent. You are worthy of sharing your knowledge and expertise with the world. Don't be so humble that you are just moping around. Being submissive and nonassertive in all areas of your life does not serve humanity well either. Embrace the balance. Sometimes you will be knocked off your high horse and life will humble you. Learn the lesson in humility and build new strategies to your level of healthy pride. It was a dose of humble pie when after teaching power yoga at a Christian yoga studio for a few years to withdraw myself from teaching. There is no telling why the attendance slowly decreased. I pride myself in teaching a strong class. Total body strength is my jam. But when the attendance slowly dropped to zero for a couple of weeks, I knew my style had to be adjusted. Teach all the modifications because strength is relative; no one wants to feel like a failure after an exercise class. I had to adjust. I had to put my pride down at this studio and adjust my style, even though the same style is appreciated and waitlisted in another studio. Study yourself and study your environment. Be flexible in your expertise. Check your ego. Ego will blame the "other," instead of having you adjust. Ego and pride will keep you believing you are an expert when there is so much growth and learning to do. Ego and pride will keep you stuck and put a cap on your growth. Humility in its unhealthy form can lead to shame and lack of confidence in your ability. Mix, balance, and check on yourself often. Your ego is your greatest enemy. Check.

JOY AND SORROW

Joy is a feeling of great pleasure and happiness. Joy and happiness are wonderful feelings to experience, but are very different.

Joy comes when you make peace with who you are, why you are, and how you are, whereas happiness tends to be externally triggered and is based on other people, things, places, thoughts, and events. Having joy includes feeling good cheer and a vibrant happiness.

Joy, in its fuller, spiritual meaning of expressing God's goodness, involves more. It is a deep-rooted, inspired happiness. The Holy Bible says, "The joy of the Lord is your strength" (Nehemiah 8:10).

Sorrow is a feeling of deep distress caused by loss, disappointment, or other misfortune suffered by oneself or others. Sorrow is a more intense form of sadness, which is the basic feeling of unhappiness.

Psychologists think sadness is a state of unhappiness while sorrow is a sense of deep distress, disappointment, or sadness.

The question is: Can sorrow and joy exist in the same space at the same time? What is the balance to this duality? There is no doubt we live in a fallen world. The headlines of the news at any particular time is proof that there will always be senselessness among us. Ninety percent of the time, the cases of murder, rape, abuse, racism, and hunger will make the news more than any good deed. There are plenty of reasons to be sorrowful on any given day, yet deeply rooted joy is the goal of a lifetime. What is the work that is needed to keep joy in a world full of sorrow?

My big plan is twofold.

1. Immersion of joy
2. Avoidance of sorrow

IMMERSION OF JOY

Joy comes from making peace with who, whose, and how you are, deeply and truthfully. Happiness is a great feeling, but joy is where the gold is. Happiness is external, the feeling of getting a new car, shoes, or purse—and it can be given and taken away. The plan is to have joy. Joy is not automatic. The work to find the joy that is within must be done. Most people of faith have the foundation of the source of their joy. Identity that is immovable with circumstances. Faith, family, and character traits are some of the immovable foundations. Not to be too technical or square, but the self-study here is well worth doing. When my feet are shaky and the world proves to be unreliable, I find myself reciting my foundation back to myself to invoke joy from within:

I, Andrea Adebambo Olatunji, am a child of the most high God. I am loved by God with characters of God. Though I walk through the valley of death, I am confident. I am bold. Greater is who and what is inside of me than anything outside of me. I am generous in kindness, love, peace, gentleness, patience, and self-control. What is for me will find me. All things that happen to me will work out for good because I love God and His creation. My peace is not given by the world and cannot be taken by the world. My path is carefully orchestrated from above.

All my gifts are from God. Born into greatness. Married to greatness.

Birthing greatness. Surrounded by greatness. I have the eyes, ears, and mind for greatness. Rise. Shine. Be God in every situation.

I have inscribed these affirmations to my heart. I magnify it to be bigger than situations that come and go. So when my husband, children, friends, work, or finances are being great OR not, I put all things under the umbrella of who and whose I am. It helps me to expect better and hope for brighter days even in my dark moments.

When the world treats me great for my status or achievements, it does not go to my head. Simultaneously when the world treats me ugly, it does not go to my heart. The power is not placed in the world standard. I need a higher being to be my source; all the other things are resources. You cannot trust resources; they give you happiness and that comes and goes. Whether you like what happens to you or not, trust the source. The determination of Romans 8:28 in the Bible is, all things will work itself out…for your good, even in death, tragedy, disease, divorce, pains, church, and inequality. Not all things are good, but all things can be good. I have seen the poor experience joy by trusting the source, and I have seen millionaires in distress because they trust the resources. There is no rhyme or rhythm to how life will happen. Trust the source! His ways are not our ways and his thinking is not our human thinking. The author of life can call a life full and complete at 9, 19, or 99. Do your part in life. Trust the source. The author of life writes the story of the beginning and the end; he adds and subtracts characters along the way. The moment the sperm meets the egg is not my timing, and the last breath is not mine either. But in the middle, I can trust the timing, characters, plot twists, triumph, sorrows, disasters, disappointments, and pain. The source can be trusted. Joy comes from that. Deeply. Truly. Great pleasure. Joy.

AVOIDANCE OF SORROW

You and I are limited resources. The bandwidth to hold emotions has a capacity. There are some things that happen to us that are within our control. There are some sorrows in our community that we can help alleviate. There are so many ways that we can serve humanity under our roofs, in our schools, in our community, in our nation, and in our world. We must focus on what we can do. I find that I am paralyzed when I ingest all the disasters of the world and have no solutions to them. I start to point fingers to other people, races, nationality, and politicians. Observe the headline news and notice what you feel. Are you indifferent, numb, sad, or overwhelmed? I was a news junkie until I noticed that the news is a business itself. It captured me and my feelings of helplessness. I know I like to stay informed, but I choose to be intentional with the news and the sorrows it brings. I want to use my energy for the change that is impactful, not be crippled by the information overload. I allow myself to feel unhappiness in any circumstance that calls for it. That's a reasonable human response. There are hormones that play a part in our moods. Serotonin regulates our mood and there are lifestyle changes that can boost and keep the hormones regulated. These are all important. Use all the tools available to keep the sorrows at bay.

Limit the intake of sorrowful, uncontrollable information. Get some healthy doses of vitamin D sunshine from the late morning. Add movement to your body, most days of the week. Be around people who add joy into your world as often as you can. You do what you can do to reduce the soil that sorrow lands on in your soul. Be intentional in doing your share to nurture the soil of your soul. You have to be intentional. Happenstance will not pull out the weed in your soul. You must develop strategies for yourself and your environment. Tend to the garden of your soul. Pull the weeds that can turn into uncontrolled sadness, sorrow, and depression. You must be proactive in protecting your soul. It is not selfish at all, guarding your mind and spirit is actually necessary to enable you to serve your world that needs you desperately to be well, whole, and joyful.

BALANCE ACT: SORROW AND JOY

Now that we know joy and sorrow, can they coexist? Yes. And at the same time. When I lost my dad, of course, I was sad beyond words because of the love I have for him. But I had equally intense joy for the life he lived. He was 92. But then I had dinner with a friend who lost her husband to cancer. I was curious to take a peep into her mind as she talked about her loss, love, joy, and tears. She was grateful to have been given the opportunity to love him for five years. Even though the loss and the sorrow were great, joy remained. Seek out this very important balance. Life happens, but you must live in established joy. Establish your joy now. Your mind might be too feeble to grasp deep joy during a crisis. Do the continuous work now.

Affirm yourself of your worth that is within now. Attach a character of God to it. Look in the mirror. Pay compliments to some things you cannot see.

If you have six-pack abs, attach God's strength to it. If you have a belly, attach God into it. You are God's temple to be honored. Attach God to be the anchor of your strength and your weaknesses. You are in this world, but your mind will know that you are more than the eye can see, you are not of the world. These are not religious jargons. These are affirmations that will give you wings even on the cloudiest of days. Personalize your joy.

JUDGMENT AND OPEN-MINDED

I find that more than ever, I must practice the duality of staying open-minded and passing judgment. We all pass judgment; we just don't admit it because it's not a trait we are proud of. What I pass judgment on and my litmus test for the future must be different. Even though my core values are solid and established for myself, I must be open to the experiences of others and not shun the world simply because we disagree on perspectives. I know I have to expand my mind to expose it to what I have not allowed in the past. Morality is important to me, but I have met great people with morality unlike mine. And I have met mean people with morality similar to mine. In 2021 and beyond, humanity will demand something different from me. After my second and third pregnancies, I was motivated to get in shape by the young, black, energetic, and handsome Shaun T. I just loved his energy. It helped me to be consistent with my workouts in between naps and breastfeeding. The awareness of my level of Catholic/religious girl judgment and self-righteousness came to me when I realized that Shaun T was gay and I lost interest in his workout programs. My husband brought my mindset to my awareness when I was bitching and bellyaching about a grown man's sexuality. He reminded me of how a couple of weeks ago, I was bragging about how much I loved him and showing off my abs from Shaun T's 25-minute workouts. "Why do you care who he loves? What if someone judges you for loving me?" I was ready with all the God disapproves homosexuality verbiage. He came back with, "Does the same Bible you read tell you not to judge others, so you will not be judged? Does it not tell you to, 'Above all, LOVE your neighbor as yourself?' If you don't love your neighbor, you do not truly love yourself." I had no comeback. I saw myself just as my husband intended for me to see. Judgmental. When you know better, do better. I was willing to be open-minded.

Open-minded: willing to consider new ideas; unprejudiced. Acknowledging that there is work for me to do. A mindset shift. Someone else's lifestyle or culture is not mine to demoralize.

Judgmental is a negative word to describe someone who often rushes to judgment without reason. The adjective judgmental describes someone who forms lots of opinions—usually harsh or critical ones—about lots of people. Judgmental types are not open-minded or easygoing. The future is going to require a balance of healthy judgment and lots of open-mindedness. You don't know what you don't know.

Psychologists say people can become judgmental due to their pride, their hurt and anger at being wronged, and a lack of love for others. Judgment can be based on race, gender, sexuality, career, nationality, or appearance. You must leave some room for growth and evolution. Just because your generation believed something for centuries does not necessarily make it right. You can open your mind to learning, loving, and reflecting on the consequences and effects of the recipient of your judgment.

Ways to overcome being judgmental include self-reflection, forgiveness, and seeing the whole person.

Being judgmental speaks more of your character than of the recipient of your judgment. Being open-minded does not open the floodgate of shift in your own standard. You can uphold your own personal standard while giving room for others with different experiences and preferences to live. Live and let others live. You are not God. God is kind enough to release us from the burden of judging others. But he did not release us from loving them. "Mind your own business" is the interpretation I am going with. The Creator mandated love. Go do that. God is not petty like us. He knows what he knows and our human brain cannot fathom all there is to know. Let the Creator handle his own creation. Show up with love. "Mind your own business" is a lifelong work. Judge that. These parables Jesus spent hours on make sense the more you live. "Why are you worried about a speck in your neighbor's eye when there is a whole log in yours?" JESUS! Shady and real. He pretty much said, Mind your own business, every day, every moment. Don't worry about the fault you find in others. Do you, Boo!

So many lies and hate are spread in the name of religion. Mind your business. Love others. Love God. Simple enough. It will take the rest of your life to master. Go do that. Actively.

LOVE IT AND LEAVE IT.

I love quotes. Good quotes can preach to my soul forever and I have sometimes navigated my thoughts with the wisdom of a great random anonymous quote. "If you love something, let it go." There is a funny addendum and amendment to this quote that I have seen on social media. "If you love someone, let them go. If they come back to you, let them go again because that means nobody else loves them." I find that funny all the time.

The concept of this duality is to not force. You can change the nature of any relationship at any time. There is no rule that ties you to be loyal to heartache, abuse, or even mere rudeness. There is nothing more powerful than the ability to change your mind.

Some people by nature are more loyal than others. I am one of those. I have done business with the same phone company, bank, and financial planner since 1999. Consistency to a pattern, person, or tradition is an excellent trait to have until you stay consistent to what does not serve you well any longer. It gets to a point where you are stuck in the old pattern. Just like an electronic device, it is healthy to do an update to your systems. This is probably the hardest mindset shift for me. Old habits are hard to break. I for sure am not changing my phone number to a new one. What if someone wants to reach me from 1999? Bogus. If the company you are loyal to doesn't bend over backward for you, permission to leave is granted. Imagine all the good services vying for your attention while you tie your loyalty to indifference.

There are plenty of options that we are blinded to when we are narrow-minded about what we will "always" or "never" do. One thing to remember is that just because someone or something does not serve you well anymore, it doesn't mean you should defame or demonize it.

2020 was a great aha! year. The forced changes to the way of life due to the COVID-19 pandemic gave me plenty of time to reflect on what is good, better, or best for me. When there is a best option, I decided to find the power, discipline, and courage to choose that. What I am noticing is that it is actually easier on my mind once I release the attachment I have to things, places, or people. There is more love to life than forcing.

At this point of our journey, you know that I am a deeply spiritual person. I am always in awe of God for His creation of this galaxy—the sunrise and unfailing sunset, stars, ocean, mountains, not to mention us, humans. I am in awe of the complexity of our brains, all our systems, digestion, circulation, and so forth working together, the rhythm of the heartbeat and breathing. I love the role of the trinity, God the father, God the son, God the Holy Spirit. I lean to each one differently. I enjoy church because of the like-minded, unforced common faith. I love serving my community in that setting—giving, loving, and sharing. When the leader of the church community started to see the world differently, his evolution was in direct contrast to my evolution. His passion was against my core values. He brought his politics unapologetically to the pulpit. Cussing, screaming, and blushing to get his point across. I gave him an A+ for passion no doubt, but the season of going along to get along was over for me. He was speaking to a lot of people, but I was no longer one of them. What I noticed was that I was losing my awestruck wonder of the God I love because of His representation on the pulpit. I started to look at all religious gatherings as phony. I lost my taste for any community of believers. I looked at them all as a corrupt, money-grabbing bunch. Letting one person change the core of who I am is a heavy price. I stepped away for a period of time to reevaluate and redefine my role if any in organized religion. My relationship with God is sacred to me. Reassigning boundaries and responsibilities for myself in any future entanglement with the church gave me new freedom to explore. The journey to rediscover newness in the old is the refresh button I needed. One bad apple should not leave you dejected; there are plenty of fish in the ocean. Imagine being stuck on the rotten one.

The same goes for relationships, careers, and friendships. Being stuck in a job you hate will have you hating the entire profession.

Change jobs before you declare that your field is trash.

Change your friend circle before you declare all friendships are evil.

Change your follower-ship before you declare social media is wicked.

Change your habits before you declare that life is foul.

You have the power to change your mind, role, and level of involvement. Take a break from any routine if it is becoming a burden. Evaluate often. A friend texted me to ask why I blocked her husband from social media. She was wondering if I had a problem with them. I calmly told her that I really like her and her husband in person and I would like to keep it that way. Everyone has freedom of speech, but his radical speech on social media was creating an unrest in my soul. My job is to guard my soul, not argue to agree or disagree on any issues. The only way to preserve love in this case was to block him. Out of sight, out of mind. That is my boundary and I am entitled to it as much as he is entitled to his thoughts. But his thoughts will not have room in my head.

The fear of "What if I change my mind?" is a real thing. Evolution is constant. That is why constant reflection is essential to growth. Change is inevitable; growth is optional. I choose growth. If I grow out of this thought process, then so be it. I will embrace the next chapter on and on until my final breath.

AUDIENCE OF ONE AND AUDIENCE OF NONE

I like to post daily on Instagram. It is not tedious for me; I actually enjoy it. Over the years, it has become my journal and reminder of what my mindset was or the events that excite or traumatize me. Every now and then, I will skip posting because I was not in the mood or I was too busy. On those days, I find myself thinking, the world of IG will miss me. The importance we place on ourselves sometimes—I post to inspire, but nobody is sitting in their little room waiting for a post from me. It is great to believe that what we have to say is important and life changing to at least one, but to also know that people are not thinking about us as much as we think they are. Everyone has their own stuff to sort through. The need to be seen and validated on and offline is a great new adjustment into the future. This need can be crippling if not adjusted. Put whatever information, value, or content that you are called or anointed to put into the world. That's it. Put it out as service to the world and take your expectations away from feedback. I get to practice this on Instagram, but it is applicable also in committees, PTA, work, and so on—put it out and don't be bugged by the likes and comments. Forget the audience feedback and focus on the audience of ONE: God. This is not to super-spiritualize anything. But it gives you a level of carefree if it is received well or not. My intention needs no validation. I have friends who are afraid to post for the fear of the feedback or no feedback. Deliver your goods and turn around in the runway of badassery; make your statement with no addendums.

It will help, inspire, or motivate one person. That is the only reason I am able to finally put clicks on this keyboard. When I was worried about how many people will find this book helpful, I was crippled by fear. But once I release it to the audience of ONE, it is on and popping. I wake up at 4:00 a.m. and I get to editing, writing, and become heavily motivated. Doing anything for the masses changes the persona; it becomes a performance, but doing it for ONE keeps me grounded, truthful, and authentic. That is the approach I take when I teach yoga. Once I look around and make eye contact with the yogi, it is authentic to the soul.

Perform for ONE, knowing that even if it is not a hit, it is done well and with a genuine, authentic spirit.

Live for the audience of ONE. It keeps the integrity of everything. It helps you to be truthful in private and public. It creates an honest life. No need to be one person in the office and another in your home. An audience of ONE is the real thing. It gives room for being tired, excited, cranky, moody, or kind. You can always embrace all the parts of you however they show up when your audience is for ONE.

Thinking of my ONE audience helps me the most when I am tired. Tiredness makes me cranky and impatient with a tendency to fly off the handle. Most times, my kids are the ones who want a little more of me at this time. When I think of my audience of ONE, it helps me take a breath and ask for time to rest before I can meet the demands asked of me. Simply acknowledging my state of mind has also inspired me to get up and continue the task. Living for an audience of ONE has helped me to offer less apologies because there are less offenses. I became a better wife, mom, daughter, sister, friend, and human.

Once, my 7-year-old kicked an opponent in anger and frustration during a soccer game. If I consider all the eyes on her and me as she behaved badly, I tend to overreact to perform for the other parents. I would have made the moment about me and how embarrassed I was for my child's choice in behavior. When I showed up just for her and an audience of ONE that sees me as I parent this child. I am gentler and more thoughtful in my discipline approach. This self-imposed concept has given me the eye to be kind to strangers, my loved ones, to reach out to the needy, to be generous beyond myself.

Stay true. Connect with your real true authentic self. Live for an audience of ONE.

REMEMBER THE DETAILS; SUMMARY DISMISSES THE WONDERS.

A few years ago, my parents came to visit. I casually asked them to write me an autobiography of their lives. Dad was so excited to jump on the project right away. In less than 24 hours, he handed me the hand-written details of his life, from birth to present. It was nine decades of living in two pages. This impromptu project brought him to tears. He cried as he mentioned his dad's name. He had not mentioned his name in years. It was therapeutic for him. Later on as we sat in my kitchen for lunch, I brought out his autobiography and asked some specific questions as I read over his written words. He was happy to elaborate. This simple exercise gave us hours and hours of conversations. He was in awe of his own life story when he allowed himself to go back to the details: the pain, the lessons, the joy, the love, the harshness, the tenderness, and all of the emotions. He was so grateful for the trip down memory lane. He made a couple of phone calls to a few of his friends who were alive to share some of the memories with them. The joy he was experiencing over reflecting on his past gave me so much comfort when I read the letter afresh, even after his passing.

In yoga, warrior 2 is a standing pose where you extend one hand forward, and the other hand extends behind you, your body is aligned in the middle, shoulders on hips, and your gaze facing forward. This pose reminds me about one of the key principles of yoga asana practice:

the balance and steadiness and ease. It also teaches us to involve the whole body in asana, and to remember that which is out of sight. Ever since my dad wrote his autobiography, I started to remind myself and other yogis to gently look back in your warrior stance and then forward. Looking back not to forget the gems of the past in our haste to grasp the future. The details of the past hold some keys to the future. What got you here that needs to be amplified, magnified, or diminished? What habits of the past are a common denominator of you that must be acknowledged for the future? There is always a pattern to you. I have been soaking up some time basking in the past, not to stay there, but for the purpose of reinventing my future.

The more I live, the more I find value in details. As a mom, it's so easy to jump from the baby stories to voila, perfect adults raised. I want to capture the details. The ugly days make the beautiful days more meaningful. I love a well-polished picture with filters and proper lighting, but don't forget to capture the real moments and process that is seen only by you. There is value in it. My family loves a trip to the Florida beaches and they cannot wait to go back as often as our schedules will allow. All they remember is the destination. The beautiful sugar-white sand, the breeze of the ocean, delicious seafood, and endless indulgences. What they often forget is the 12-hour road trip to and from Texas—the whining, the frustrations, the games played, the hugs, the fights among siblings, and the meals at questionable restaurants along the way. Years after the trips when I share the road trip experiences, they appreciate the journey just as much as the beautiful destinations. Take time to sit in the details of your story. Sometimes go back and read your old journals just to appreciate the growth that has taken place over the years.

I don't want to go back to live in the past along with all its pain or sadness, but I sure don't want to forget the strength that I acquired along the way. It would be a great loss if you didn't allow yourself to reflect in detail and meditate on the ups, downs, and all the in-betweens.

A crisis is a terrible thing to waste.

My friend Lisa, a wonderful, pleasant, and goal-oriented woman in her mid-forties, is considering marriage for the third time. The first two marriages started out in a fairy tale kind of fantasy but ended bitterly. She excitedly told me over lunch how her current boyfriend is the "one" and they are considering making things official with a marriage ceremony. Not to dampen the mood, but I couldn't help but be honest with my friend. The end of the last relationship just a couple of years prior was ugly, painful, and downright dramatic. I asked her, "What will make this one different?" She blurted out how she loves him. Since we already made a pact to be completely honest, I said, "but you loved the last guy." I knew I was killing the vibe, but I asked her to go down memory lane and reflect on what went wrong with the last two husbands. What will be different this time? Have you sought out therapy? Counseling? Who were you in the last relationship that you are not now? What skills do you have now that you did not have before? Why do you want this now? I promised to support whatever her decisions will be, but I encouraged her to spend some time in her old journal and find her role in the last relationships and how the future might resemble her past based on unresolved patterns. Only time will tell if the lessons of the past helps or hurts the future, but we must be honest with ourselves to ask the questions.

You are the common denominator in every experience you are in. Only you have the power to change yourself. You can influence change in others, but, ultimately, all you have is you.

The biblical story of the Israelites is a reminder for me of how forgetting the past will have you doing the same things over and over, and expecting a different result is a clear definition of insanity.

The Israelites were slaves in Egypt for centuries. They were released from slavery through a series of miracles, given specific directions about what to do and how to do it to get to a land promised to them flowing with milk and honey. They kept doing things on impulse, forgetting the suffering of the past, and they lost track of a future ahead. They at one point craved slavery, the same slavery that was the most horrible for them.

We are no different than the Israelites. If we are not mindful, we will forget all the details of the past and simply crave the highlights.

Make yourself remember the details of how far you've come. Brag on yourself for the courage, strength, resilience, and self-love that got you here and propel some wisdom into your own future.

Every tool we desire for the future is already within us. The tools we are craving can be found in our history, roots, and patterns.

May we find the courage to explore and awaken the giant within. The magic is already within; explore it and propel into your future.

Namaste and Amen.

CPSIA information can be obtained
at www.ICGtesting.com
Printed in the USA
BVHW042224160821
614548BV00019B/621